CLASSIC
AMERICA

CLASSIC AMERICA

THE FEDERAL STYLE
&
BEYOND

WENDELL GARRETT

PRINCIPAL PHOTOGRAPHY BY PAUL ROCHELEAU

RIZZOLI
NEW YORK

For Betsy
with love

"More is thy due than more than all can pay."
SHAKESPEARE, *Macbeth*, Act I, Scene 4, Line 21

First published in the United States of America in 1992 by
RIZZOLI INTERNATIONAL PUBLICATIONS, INC.
300 Park Avenue South, New York, New York 10010

Library of Congress Cataloging-in-Publication Data

Garrett, Wendell D.
Classic America : the Federal style and beyond / by Wendell Garrett.
p. cm.
Includes bibliographical references and index.
ISBN 0-8478-1585-4
1. Architecture. Domestic—Atlantic States. 2. Neoclassicism
(Architecture)—Atlantic States. 3. Interior architecture—Atlantic
States. 4. Decoration and ornament—Atlantic States—Neoclassicism.
I. Title.
NA7206.G37   1992
728'.0974—dc20   92-5577
CIP

Design by David Larkin

Printed and bound in Japan

CONTENTS

No. III.

A SERPENTINE KNEE-HOLE LIBRARY WRITING TABLE,

Four feet long, two feet fix inches wide, nine drawers in front, cock beaded, an aftragal or ftone moulding on the edge of the top, on faft plinth - - - 3 6 0

EXTRAS.

	£.	s.	d.
Each inch, more or lefs, in length or width		1	0
Ditto, with double front		1	3
Making ditto in three carcafes		3	0
Each drawer, more or lefs		2	9
Each partition			
Lining ditto crofs-way,		1	0
Veneering drawer fronts, each			
Veneering partition edges afkew or crofs-way, per foot extra			
Sweeping with king, tulip, or any other hard wood, at per foot			
When both fronts are made ferpentine, and plain veneering ditto in the length, and a cupboard in each wing of one front,		10	6
Sweeping the ends half ferpentine, the other front as in the preamble, extra			
When both fronts are made ferpentine, with three drawers in the length,	18		0
Sweeping the ends ferpentine, plain veneer'd		15	
For the price of canted corners or columns—See Serpentine Dreffing Cheft.			

An aftragal on the front and ends of the carcafe, when the ends are ftraight

Ditto, when the ends are half ferpentine

Ditto, when a double front and ftraight ends

Ditto, when ferpentine ends

Each extra miter, when canted corners

Sawing drawer fronts out of two-inch ftuff,

Ditto three-inch ftuff

Glueing up ditto, at per joint

For the price of extra work—See No. 2.

Oiling and polifhing, when a fingle front

Ditto, when a double front

A CIRCULAR LIBRARY

THREE feet fix inches diameter, and four ... run in fquare, and ... top to turn round on ... ten'd to ditto by ... claws as No ...

Federalist New England and the New Nation

Opposite

The London price book for cabinetwork of 1797 and tools of the cabinetmaker's trade. The late eighteenth century was a golden age for English-speaking American culture, when American furniture reached a consistency of design and quality never achieved before or since. "Embellishments," as Franklin noted, were replacing mere comfort in the homes of the rich; comfort was supplanting privation in the houses of the not-so-rich. Yeoman farmers, urban craftsmen, merchants, and planters were building a prosperous and productive society. In constructing houses and making furniture, these accomplished amateurs followed the latest pattern books from England. In all those books design was controlled by the same preoccupation with order and proportion echoed in much of the painting, literature, and music of the time.

WITH THE SIGNING of the Peace of Paris in 1783, twenty years of protest and war came suddenly to a close. Between the end of the War of Independence and Thomas Jefferson's ideal of the new republic of 1801, America became a modern nation. In late 1782, with the adoption of the Great Seal of the United States with the Latin phrase *novus ordo seclorum*, the Confederation Congress officially proclaimed that a "new order of the ages" had arrived and a new historical era was at hand. In fact, the announcement implied something even greater—not simply the coming of a modern age, but the creation of an entirely new way of thinking about history itself.

Most of the new nation's leaders were versed in history in the conventional sense: the history of ancient Greece and Rome, of confederations and republics, and of England, at least since Elizabethan times. In structuring a self-constituting and self-sustaining republic, most of them thought historically, using references to ancient or modern history to support or illustrate their reasoning. Equally, the public men in America were acutely conscious of history in another sense, that of their place in its ongoing flow of unprecedented nation building, providing an example to be emulated by emerging nations throughout the world for hundreds of years to come. "You and I, my dear friend," John Adams wrote to Richard Henry Lee of Virginia in 1777, "have been sent into life at a time when the greatest lawgivers of antiquity would have wished to live. How few of the human race have ever enjoyed an opportunity of making election by government . . . for themselves and their children." By 1787 the euphoria Adams expressed had given way to a sense of urgency. It was "more than probable," James Madison said in the Constitutional Convention, that the delegates "were now digesting a plan which in its operation would decide forever the fate of Republican Government." Even after the Convention had successfully completed its work, Washington declared in his Inaugural Address that "the sacred fire of liberty and the destiny of the republican model of government" were deeply and irrevocably staked "on the experiment intrusted to the hands of the American people." This period can be seen as a time when a transformation was taking place—America's "Machiavellian moment," to borrow J.G.A. Pocock's phrase—the time when citizens, acting consciously and with intention, created a new and enduring order, the decisive moment when a people became aware of its mortality and took steps to confront it with human initiative.

In their reading of the past, eighteenth-century American statesmen tended to look at history as a storehouse of examples, any one of which could be lifted out of time and placed in the present, and they tended to combine the sacred and the secular. Many held a covenant theory of history in which God periodically anointed certain nations as his chosen people. According to the Bible, Abraham had passed this national covenant to his children, who comprised the nation of Israel. It was argued that from Israel the covenant had been transferred to the first Christians, who in turn had passed it to the early modern Protestants of Europe and England; it was carried to the New World by the Puritans. American Protestants began to describe themselves as the chosen people of God—the "American Israel."

By the end of the eighteenth century, certain rationalists began to formulate an alternative, secular reading of history. They claimed the germ of civilization from ancient Israel had been passed to the city-states of fifth-century Greece, and with the Greeks civilization had come into its full glory. In Montesquieu's *Spirit of Laws* they found the Greek polis of the Periclean Age presented as a republican prototype, a perfect civilized state that had combined an abiding respect for personal liberty with a strong commitment to public service, a model for ages to come. This secular history was neither continuous nor cumulative, but cataclysmic, with reason leaping from one civilization to the next, the light of learning suddenly blazing forth from darkness. The course of civilization went from Greece to Rome where, following the fall of the Alexandrian empire, the spirit of the liberal arts and sciences rose again. Over time, however, the love of learning was lost, and Roman republicans grew slothful and profligate. A series of despots further sapped the spirit of the Roman people. By the fourth century, Roman civilization had grown too corrupt to defend itself from the barbarian invaders who struck the final blow. Eighteenth-century Americans showed a peculiar fascination with the Dark Ages, which they viewed as a long night of ecclesiastical and feudal tyranny that had followed the fall of Rome, but they were equally fascinated by the advent of modern times, which they attributed to the Renaissance. The progress of knowledge and the advances in the liberal arts and sciences during the Renaissance were only preparatory to the most significant development: the discovery of the New World. America had been discovered and explored through the aid of scientific inventions; it had been colonized and settled by educated, rational people. In other words, America symbolized the rebirth of civilization.

Citizens of the new republic found comfort in viewing themselves as fundamentally different from their European progenitors. They were members of a liberal society happily free of feudal traditions and class distinctions and committed to individual expression, social mobility, pragmatic self-interest, and protection of property rights. Americans assumed that their nation was descended from both ancient Israel and the classical civilizations: America had both a mythic and mundane past, a sacred and secular heritage. A dizzying variety of preachers and cultural critics proclaimed this theme. In sermons, ministers spoke of creation—the miraculous founding of America, its unique world character, its primordial innocence—turning for their text to the passage from Isaiah: "Shall the earth be made to bring forth in a day? Shall a nation be brought forth at once?" In a single sentence John Adams summed up the American mission as an empire of both religion and rationality: "I always consider the settlement of America with reverence and wonder, as the opening of a grand scene and design in Providence for the illumination of the ignorant, and the emancipation of the slavish part of mankind all over the earth." America was the New World embodiment of both the Reformation and the European Enlightenment. "The foundation of our empire," Washington wrote at the end of the war in his Circular Letter to the state governors, "was not laid in the gloomy age of ignorance and superstition." It had been deferred to be founded in an age of enlightened reason. As a result, its citizens could call upon the "treasures of knowledge, acquired by the labors of philosophers, sages, and legislators" for their use, and with this store of learning they had a "fairer opportunity for political happiness, than any other nation has ever been favoured with." In the eyes of the Revolutionary republicans, the new nation was to be an example for the rest of the world, a beacon of liberty.

What reason was there to believe that America could flout history and defy logic by this bold experiment in self-government, formulated on a scale and with a vigor unprecedented in history? To convert a continent into a republic, said a skeptical Patrick Henry, was "a work too great for human wisdom." Yet with touching faith, these remarkable political leaders dreamed of an American Athens and proclaimed a flowering of the arts and the immediate arrival of the muses; cultural nationalists assumed that the people at large would eagerly support artists, poets, and playwrights who would soon rival the ancients. On the eve of the American Revolution, Horace Walpole predicted, "The next Augustan Age will dawn on the other side of the Atlantic.

10

There will perhaps be a Thucydides at Boston, Xenophon at New York, and in time a Virgil in Mexico, and a Newton in Peru." In 1790 James Wilson of Philadelphia observed that when the histories of the United States were written, America would compare favorably "with the most illustrious commonwealths, which adorn the records of time." He continued, "When some future Xenophon or Thucydides shall arise to do justice to their virtues and their actions, the glory of America will rival—it will outshine the glory of Greece." These were extravagant assumptions, to be sure, but as Thomas Paine observed, "The sun never shined on a cause of greater worth."

By 1790 the United States had a relatively prosperous but fundamentally underdeveloped economy supporting a population of 4,000,000 in a narrow band of farmland that extended from the St. Lawrence Valley to the border of Florida, which was still under Spanish rule. Not one in ten lived in a town of a thousand inhabitants, and almost everyone outside these towns was a farmer. American provincialism was intense, roads were few and in abominable condition, and communication between towns and villages was slight. Outside the great seaports, competition was dormant and enterprise stifled. Commercially the Americans needed the British more than the British needed them.

New England's Maritime Economy

The outbreak of war between England and France in 1793 gave New England merchants a chance to reap soaring profits as neutral carriers between the warring parties. Massachusetts, with its long coastline and abundant good harbors, became a maritime commonwealth out of necessity. The waterside Yankees of New England were formidable profit-takers; they made money, and lost it, by buying, bartering, smuggling, shipping, and selling whatever commodity turned a profit. In their search for new markets and quick returns, New England shipmasters fanned out to ports around the Indian Ocean and in the Pacific on their way to Canton to engage in the China Trade. "Commerce occupies all their thought, turns all their heads, and absorbs all their speculations," wrote the French traveler Jacques Brissot de Warville in 1788. To Timothy Dwight, president of Yale University, Bostonians seemed "distinguished by a lively imagination. . . . Their enterprises are sudden, bold, and sometimes rash. A general spirit of adventure prevails here." They sold cod to the Roman Catholic countries of Europe, carried back the heavy wines of the Mediterranean Coasts and Atlantic islands, traded sandalwood, *bêche-de-mer* or trepang, a type of sea cucumber, and sea otter pelts in Canton, and even engaged in the slave trade. Profits entailed risks, and Yankee ships were sunk on coral reefs, lost in tropical storms, burned by disgruntled natives, seized by pirates, and destroyed by British and French men-of-war. The ocean knows no favorites and a mariner's life was a dangerous calling, as many of Salem's more than 400 widows in 1783 would have testified.

The impact of the exotic imports from the Far East on Boston—the Athens of America if not the hub of the universe, as Bostonians liked to think of their town—was palpable and startling. Van Wyck Brooks noted, "The Cushing house on Summer Street was surrounded with a wall of Chinese porcelain. Peacocks strutted about the garden. The Chinese servants wore their native dress." Boston's most formidable rival in maritime commerce was Salem, which in 1790 was the sixth largest city in the United States with nearly 8,000 inhabitants. The *Grand Turk* of Salem was the first Massachusetts vessel to reach the Far East, and her return in May 1787 brought fabulous profits to her owner, Elias Hasket Derby. Her voyage challenged the ingenuity and energy of every Massachusetts mariner to sail "to the farthest port of the rich East," as Salem's municipal seal proclaims. By 1804 Salem was in full flower as a busy, prosperous, and cosmopolitan seaport of 10,000 inhabitants, most of whom made their living from the sea. For half a mile along Salem's harbor front runs Derby Street, with the long finger of Derby Wharf extending into the harbor in front of the Custom House, the residential and business center of town in the early nineteenth century. On one side were the brick and frame mansions of the merchant-shipowners—the Derbys, Princes, Crowninshields, and Peabodys. Opposite were the wharves, warehouses, shipyards, ship chandlers, ropewalks, and sailmakers, all seen against a background of sails, spars, and rigging. At its peak, overseas trade made Salem a city-state, trading proudly in her own right with Canton and Sumatra. So common were her ships in Far Eastern ports that one wealthy trader there "believed Salem to be a country by itself, and one of the richest and most important sections of the globe." Her leathery seamen and daring merchants lived by a rugged faith, and on their bookshelves, beside the sermons of Cotton Mather, stood Nathaniel Bowditch on navigation. Their lives were governed, as their ancestors' had been, by the vagaries of the ocean, the routine of the countinghouse, and the discipline of the Congregational meetinghouse.

By 1807 when neutral trade reached its zenith, Newburyport, a few miles north along the coast, had achieved a standard of living which all but a few of their colonial forebears would have found unbelievable. The source of most of this wealth lay in the expanding business of Newburyport's merchants and of those men who constructed and supported the town's extensive fleet. Hardly a traveler passed through Newburyport whose journal did not note the grace and charm of its domestic architecture. High Street, running the town's full length along the ridge behind the wharves and parallel to the Merrimack River, displayed an elegance unmatched in any port save Chestnut Street in Salem. Timothy Dwight, who toured New England between 1795 and 1816, found that Newburyport's houses were more impressive than those of any other town in the region. After speaking of the air of "wealth, taste and elegance" which he felt permeating the town, Dwight concluded that "few places, probably in the world, furnish more means of a delightful residence than Newburyport." The courthouse constructed on High Street opposite the head of the Green had a distinguished pedigree, for the Boston architect Charles Bulfinch drew the plans. Classical Rome had come to Newburyport with this handsome edifice, its façade incorporating an open portico on the ground level, graceful columns and arches supporting the upper story, and the pediment capped with the figure of Justice.

Robert Adam and the Federal Style

New England architecture relied to a large degree upon English neoclassicism—the ardent and very special form developed by Robert Adam who, together with his brother James, brought about the most significant revolution in English architecture since the Palladian movement. Adam's preference, in his arrangement of mass, for the alternation of contrasting but connected units, symmetrically disposed, and for the forward and backward movement of exterior planes owes much to the Palladian style. But it was in highly original interiors that Adam displayed his delicate and imaginative decoration, and these had the greatest influence on New England. Two aspects of Adam's handling of interiors are significant: the richly varied organization of his

13

spatial volumes and the extraordinary grace and elegance of his vivacious ornament. In defining interior spaces, Adam based his schemes on function and variety, rather than applying the formal principles of his Palladian predecessors. The components of buildings were still symmetrically disposed on the exterior, but within the forms of the spaces—the rectangle, the circle, and the oval—did not always correspond reciprocally around the central axis. In the ancient wall paintings at Pompeii and Herculaneum, Adam discovered a lavish and felicitous ornamental vocabulary, delicate in scale and capricious in color, developed with an inexhaustible variety of pictorial and decorative treatment. Inspired by both the spatial system and the decorative motifs of the Romans, Adam took the classical idiom and fashioned it into a style uniquely his own.

The Federal style in America, like the Adam style, was an interior style. It was based on the same attenuated proportions and drawing on the same decorative conventions, but the effect was simpler, more severe, more chaste than the British. A strong thread of the "Puritan plain style" still ran through the fabric of New England society. House plans were simpler, and ornament was thinner, flatter, even more refined. The resulting Federal style has a clean-cut, sharp-edged purity. Instead of the delicate but sparkling color of Adam's work, Americans preferred a more subtle palette of pastel colors. These deviations from the Adam style can be attributed in part to the more conservative and provincial taste of both the American client and local designer. It is more than coincidence that the Adamesque practitioners were all American local craftsmen who adapted the style primarily from pattern books. Already sharpened and made excessively linear by the nature of engraved plates, the illustrated motifs of English neoclassicism were even more finely executed in the hands of local craftsmen.

The first design books treated the Adam style as an ornamental vocabulary supplementing the older Palladian forms rather than a new style. It was accepted rather grudgingly at first in conservative rural areas, but before the turn of the century the basic Adam house form was established in New England. The quoined corners, projecting pediments, and engaged pilasters of the colonial house disappeared, leaving a modest but delicately proportioned entrance porch. Windows were more generous and taller in proportion, with larger panes and thinner sashes. With little other focus for decoration on the façade, the central doorway became more

14

elaborate, with an elliptical fanlight and sidelights subdivided by intricate patterns of wire-thin struts. The attic story and its dormer windows were replaced by a third story so that the house resembled a simple cube. This look was reinforced by flattening the roof and installing the balustrade at the cornice line, thus masking the roof shape from view. For the first time circular, elliptical, and octagonal rooms broke through the tyranny of the rectangle and pushed out in swelling curves. Rooms even had elliptical or semicircular vaults and occasionally a dome. The underlying spirit of the Federal style, North and South, was the use of the circle and the ellipse, shapes that occur again and again in room plans, staircases, and window and door openings and give the style its special grace and elegance.

Design for a house, by Robert Adam.

The principal elements of the Federal style are even more in evidence in its ornament. It is chaste, serene, and controlled. Swept clean of ornamentation, walls are smoothly plastered and painted in pastel colors or papered in small, discreet patterns. Moldings, door frames, and fireplace surrounds are covered with ornament of tiny elements—supremely rhythmic, wire-fine, and delicately scaled geometric and natural motifs drawn in elegant but circumscribed patterns. The ornamental vocabulary includes elongated colonettes and pilasters; miniature triglyphs and dentils; reeding, fluting, and beading; decorated and fluted ovals and paterae with urns, garlands, swags, palmettes, rosettes, and baskets of fruit. Roman bulls' heads and torches mingle with American eagles and sheaves of wheat.

Samuel McIntire in Salem

Samuel McIntire, wood-carver and "the architect of Salem," spent all his life in that city and within the framework of his craft and family shop. The addition of the word "architect" to his gravestone indicates his achievement as well as his aspiration. He learned his craft from his father; he never traveled; in architecture he was completely self-taught. He seems to have been content with a limited number of simple motifs, which he reworked and brought together in a variety of arrangements. Those elements he did combine were refined and related with an exquisite sense of rightness and executed with matchless skill. Despite his impeccable craftsmanship and native sense of taste and proportion, McIntire remained more the artisan and builder than the architect, dependent on pattern books and on the work of others. Yet, in the quality of his carved details and of his interiors, his decorative work stands at the summit of the Federal style.

McIntire spent his life working for wealthy and ambitious patrons of Salem. The Peirce-Nichols House, built in the early 1780s and remodeled in 1801, was his first major work and has had as interesting a social history as any Federal house in New England. The young architect's source in carving the west parlor overmantel and the details of the Doric order in the porches and pilasters of the exterior was an out-of-date pattern book by Batty Langley. As a consequence, these portions of the house do not appear to differ greatly from those in the earlier Palladian mode. The house, with bold corner pilasters and a foreshortened third story, demonstrates the architect's sound sense and understanding of proportion. The great corner pilasters are practically the only surface ornamentation; the windows are capped simply and the front and side porches are restrained and dignified. The roof is hidden by a balustrade. The tall, solid mass of the structure and the refined carving of the doorway and the urns on the gateposts place it among the outstanding houses that survive from the early Federal period.

McIntire's surviving masterpiece is the Gardner-Pingree House, built for John Gardner in 1804–05 and the home of the Pingree family for nearly a century. The building is remarkable for its combination of austerity and grace. The façade is simple to the point of being stark, but it expresses all of the dignity, restraint, and monumentality of the Federal period. The rectangle of the building is given horizontal emphasis by the stone string-courses that divide the wall into three elongated units varying in proportion from bottom to top. The gracefully flared stone lintels above the windows are set flush against the wall, which is otherwise unadorned except for the string-courses. Centered in this elegantly proportioned façade is the projecting semicircular portico, rhythmically echoing the elliptical fanlight over the door. The lavishness of the interior ornamentation surpasses all other surviving houses from this period. The plaster ornaments were probably imported from England, but they are believed to have been made from molds carved by McIntire. The sheaves of wheat, the baskets of fruit, the pierced balusters, and the reeding and fluting were carved in wood. The chaste simplicity of McIntire's work distinguishes it from the extravagant and colorful elegance of Adam style in England; in fact, this very quality of reserve reflects the residual strain of New England Calvinism that survived into the early nineteenth century.

The Federalist Era in Boston

Federalism—a state of mind rather than an era—dominated Boston after the British departed in 1776 down to about 1820. The Federalist period takes its name from the Federalist party, which elected John Adams president in 1797. But Federalism soon belied its name. While Boston had pleaded for union in 1775, by 1815 many proper Bostonians thought of breaking it up. That radical man, Jefferson, was no longer in the White House but his disciple, James Madison, was still President. It was the era of the Hartford Convention, when Massachusetts, Rhode Island, Connecticut, Vermont, and New Hampshire delegates argued for expanded powers for state legislatures, anticipating the states rights doctrine of the South in later years. If in Europe romanticism was modern, in Boston modernity was a reversion to neoclassical verse, a gloomy view of man, literary theory as public responsibility, and a cheerful sense that wining and dining produced right thinking. The Essex Junto aristocracy seemed to be shrewd sea captains, admiralty lawyers, and merchant marine proprietors. For them, President Jefferson was a mutinous first mate of the ship of state.

State Street, Boston, and the Old State House as it appeared in 1801.
MASSACHUSETTS HISTORICAL SOCIETY

Because the British held New York until 1783, Boston commerce flourished and the population increased. For several years after the Revolution it numbered less than 20,000 inhabitants, but in 1800 the census showed 25,000. In appearance, Boston resembled an English market town of crooked and narrow streets, of a kind even then old-fashioned. Its culture was conservative: thirty years later Emerson was to say that there had not been a book, a speech, or a conversation in Boston between 1790 to 1820, but he was a radical. This period was an era of paradox rather than tranquillity. The town was managed by selectmen, the elected instruments of the town meetings, whose jealousy of granting power was even greater than their resistance to spending money and whose hostility to city government was not to be overcome. The extremes and disparity of wealth and poverty of Boston's few Federalist merchants and the mass of unskilled, propertyless population— Boston's "plain people"— engaged in dockside occupations, living together in a small, crowded city on a water-restricted peninsula evoked considerable comment. Boston, said one contemporary, "exhibits a noble appearance as the spectator sails up the harbor, or approaches it from the country. This splendid exterior, however, has not a corresponding regularity and symmetry within. The city was built almost from the beginning, without any regard to plan, beauty or future convenience, and the streets were left to fashion themselves into a tortuous intricacy that might have excited the envy of Daedalus of old." Because of the arrangement of its streets, Boston consisted of several sections—exclusive of the central business district—which existed in relative isolation from one another. The north end of the city contained persons chiefly engaged in maritime and food-marketing functions. The area to the west, known as West Boston or the West End, housed a good part of the city's independent artisans, like masons and carpenters. On the north side of Beacon Hill lay the city's Negro neighborhood; on the south side were clerks, artisans, merchants, and professionals. The homes near High, Pearl, and Summer streets were monuments to successful merchants, who had a short stroll of two or three blocks to their wharfside offices. Henry Adams in his *History of the United States* said of Federalist Boston in 1800: "Wealth and population were doubling; the exports and imports of New England were surprisingly large, and shipping was greater than that of New York and Philadelphia combined; but Boston had already learned, and was to learn again, how fleeting were the riches that depended on foreign commerce, and conservative habits were not easily changed by a few years of accidental gain." Of Stephen Higginson, Boston merchant and privateer, his grandson later wrote:

He had long been one of the so-called Essex Junto; had fervently supported Washington . . . was in close correspondence with Timothy Pickering; sat constantly in counsel with George Cabot, Josiah Quincy, Harrison Gray Otis; . . . supported Fisher Ames, as the most trustworthy orator and expounder of their party declaring that society ought to be controlled by the "wise, the good, and the rich" . . . admired Hamilton and Jay, detested Jefferson and the Democrats, hated Bonaparte, dreaded French plots . . . wished for a cordial alliance with Great Britain; in a word, was a thorough-going, uncompromising, ardent, steadfast Federalist . . . in every fibre of his frame.

Charles Bulfinch, Architect

When Charles Bulfinch returned in 1787, after almost two years abroad in Europe, Boston was still a provincial town, secure in the insular fastness of the Shawmut Peninsula. Narrow winding streets crawled in a random interlace around the town cove and docks. There had been no significant construction for almost thirty years, and many of the surviving buildings were still medieval in character. When Louis Antoine de Bougainville, a French abbé and naval officer, visited Boston in 1781, he reported:

The appearance of the buildings seems strange to European eyes; being built entirely of wood, they have not the dull and heavy appearance which belongs to those of our continental cities; they are regular and well lighted, with frames well joined, and the outside covered with slight, thinly-planed boards, overlapping each other somewhat like the tiles of our roofs. The exterior is generally painted of a grayish color, which gives an agreeable aspect to the view. The furniture is simple; sometimes of costly wood, after the English fashion; the rich covering of their floors with woollen carpets or rush matting, and others with fine sand.

Thomas Pemberton, whose *Topographical and Historical Description of Boston* of 1794 was the first systematic account published, observed:

The dwelling houses in Boston have an advantage above most of the large towns on the continent with respect to garden spots. Few houses are without them, in which vegetables and flowers are raised, in some fruit trees are planted; and what is still more intrinsically good and valuable, the inhabitant is supplied with pure wholesome water from a well in his own yard.

Boston was a town in which the artisans and craftsmen were meeting a purely local demand; where shipyards, ropewalks, and sail lofts were building and outfitting local ships, and where carpenters, cabinetmakers, tailors, and butchers were engaged in housing, furnishing, clothing, and feeding their neighbors who owned and manned those ships.

The transformation which Bulfinch brought about in Boston during the thirty years between his return from Europe and his appointment as Architect of the Capitol in Washington in 1818 cannot be measured in buildings alone. Not only was Boston stamped architecturally with new qualities of dignity and elegance in useful and handsome buildings, but streets were improved and beautified by planting, park areas were projected if not actually developed, and in general higher levels of taste and sophistication prevailed. When Elias Boudinot returned to Boston in 1809 after thirty years, he wrote, "I am really astonished at the appearance of Wealth, magnificence and taste, thro'out the town." All of this had been accomplished by Charles Bulfinch. "Like the merchants of Renaissance Italy," Samuel Eliot Morison has observed, "those of Federalist Boston wished to perpetuate their names and glorify their city by mansions, churches, and public buildings of a new style and magnificence. Luckily, among their number was a young man who had the training and the genius to guide this impulse into fruitful and worthy channels. . . . Charles Bulfinch." Urbane, sophisticated, and knowledgeable, Bulfinch nonetheless had a reverence for tradition, particularly English tradition, that kept him from radical innovation. His fastidious taste created brick houses of an elegance reminiscent of the Adam brothers in London and the dignified symmetries of Bath that dominated New England architectural expression for more than a generation.

Between graduation from Harvard College in 1781 and his trip abroad, Bulfinch was employed in Joseph Barrell's counting room where, given the unsettled state of business in the early 1780s, he was—in his own words—"at leisure to cultivate a taste for Architecture." In Paris he came under the tutelage of Thomas Jefferson, who sent him to southern France and on to Italy, where he saw buildings that were a far cry from the Boston of his youth. On his return home, this young man of taste and property was, as he wrote, "warmly received by friends, and passed a season of leisure, pursuing no business but giving gratuitous advice in architecture, and looking forward to an establishment in life." Thus, he performed as a gentleman amateur, but in early 1796, through circumstances beyond his control, Bulfinch was forced to declare bankruptcy and his personal holdings were liquidated. From this point on, of necessity and by natural inclination, his practice became increasingly professional, and by the turn of the century his reputation as an architect was secure. He brought to his work qualifications that established professional standing: the use of drawings as a means for developing ideas and the active participation in the construction of buildings.

While Bulfinch was still abroad, he had heard about the building of the Charles River Bridge. This venture proved so successful that a second toll bridge, linking the west end of Cambridge Street to the opposite shore in Cambridge, opened in late 1793. Bulfinch worked extensively in the rapidly developing and increasingly handsome West End of his birth. The first Harrison Gray Otis House built on Cambridge Street in 1796, established his canon—a clean-cut cube of red brick with a sharp cornice; immaculate walls with tall, slender windows beautifully spaced; narrow horizontal white stone bands marking the story divisions; and an exquisitely rendered elliptical porch with elongated columns and pilasters in the Corinthian order. Here he retained an old-fashioned preference for the Palladian window on the second floor and what seems a consciously anachronistic insistence on the semicircular rather than the elliptical form in lunettes and fanlights. The latter feature, along with the use of a window recessed in an arch, is almost a signature of

Bulfinch design. In all, the architect designed three houses for Otis. The second, built on Mount Vernon Street in 1800, is an outgrowth of his plan for urbanizing Beacon Hill with large lots with ample room for gardens and stables. By setting the full-length windows on the ground floor in segmental wall arches and topping them with a light string-course, the architect created the effect of a basement story that carries two lighter ranges of windows above. This was a standard formula for the fashionable townhouses of London and Bath. Moreover, the slender, flat pilasters are strongly reminiscent of Adam's treatment of the end pavilions in his Adelphi Terrace. With its austere geometric walls with sharply cut openings, each sensitively proportioned and rhythmically graded from bottom to top, the second Otis house remains, after nearly two hundred years, one of the handsomest in Boston.

Harrison Gray Otis moved again in 1806 to an even larger house at 45 Beacon Street facing the Common. In actual measurement the façade forms a simple rectangle, but as seen from the street it appears tall in proportion, an impression Bulfinch created through subtle means. By spacing the windows more closely vertically than horizontally, he drew them tightly into five rising tiers. Then he accelerated this vertical movement by varying the shapes of the windows at the different floor levels. On the second or principal floor, they are full-length and triple-hung, giving them very tall and narrow proportions. The primary aspect of Bulfinch's third Otis House is its supremely beautiful attenuated proportions, which give the building its soaring vertical elegance.

As one of the most powerful figures in the Boston of his day, and as a recognized leader of the Federalist party and a founding member of the Mount Vernon Proprietors who bought the property of John Singleton Copley on Beacon Hill, Otis enjoyed a position of immense social prominence. Samuel Eliot Morison, the descendant and biographer of Otis, has said of life in the third house:

Whilst there was a certain amplitude in the Otises' way of living, it was neither extravagant nor aristocratic. . . . Those old Bostonians unashamedly enjoyed eating and drinking. While the Otis family were in residence at Number 45 Beacon Street, a blue and white Lowestoft [China Trade] punch bowl, with a capacity of over two gallons, sat every afternoon on the landing halfway to the drawing rooms, filled with punch for the benefit of visitors. . . . Family tradition is positive that his usual breakfast dish, even at the age of eighty, was a moderate-sized tureen of pâté de fois gras.

Intelligent, articulate, and possessed of wide cultural interests, he obviously lived with a zest for the finer things of life. Because of their architect and patron, the three Harrison Gray Otis mansions have become the architectural embodiment of the Federal style in New England.

One of Bulfinch's most original contributions was his proposal for the Tontine Crescent, a row of sixteen connected brick houses on Franklin Street, a design reminiscent of the Adam brothers in London and the great crescents and circuses of Bath. The graceful curve of the Crescent was an island of urban elegance and reasoned dignity in the awkward meanderings of a provincial colonial town. All of the window openings were cut sharply into the curving unbroken walls without ornamentation. Projecting prominently from the center of this main block was a central pavilion with a colonnade of two pairs of coupled Corinthian columns supporting a classical entablature and pediment. The order rose from a high basement into which was cut an arched opening which led through toward Summer Street, giving origin and name to Arch Street. The graceful curved surfaces of the main walls stretched left and right until they reach the last two house units on either end, the terminating pavilions of the design which were made to project slightly and were adorned with pilasters. The Tontine Crescent (built 1793–94; demolished 1858) was a triumphant success at first and widely praised, but in the end it proved to be a personal disaster for the architect. With the worsening economic conditions in Boston that preceded the ratification of Jay's Treaty in 1794, opening British ports in both the East and West Indies to American trade, Bulfinch's involvement in the project brought about his bankruptcy.

By the early 1790s the state government had outgrown the old Town House, which had through the eighteenth century accommodated both town and provincial governments and the courts. In 1793 the Boston town meeting approved a plan to buy from John Hancock's heirs the late governor's pasture on the slope of Beacon Hill above the Common as a site for a new building. Officially opened in early 1798 the new Massachusetts State House was the crowning achievement of Bulfinch's early years. It was derivative in its dependence on Sir William Chambers's Somerset House in London, the central portion of which was finished in 1786 while Bulfinch was still there. Chambers's design substantially influenced the elevation of Bulfinch's façade, from the arcaded basement to the dome, and in the lateral wings one encounters once more the familiar Palladian window set into a recessed wall arch. Yet the State House is, in fact, more Adamesque than its London prototype. It is more austere and simpler, reflecting its provincial origins. The Boston architect eliminated Chambers's heavy rustication and used clean flat walls of brick discreetly divided by thin, white string-courses. Window and door openings were sharply cut and unadorned. The clean brick piers, spaced to correspond to the coupled and single columns they carry, assert their function as vertical supports without the interruption of surface ornament. Each of these lines of vertical force rests upon a sequence of equally unadorned piers and brick arches. Even though the sources of the components are obvious, Bulfinch has so thoroughly thought out the attenuated proportions, the delicate scale, and the part-to-part relationships that they attain an innate sense of formal rightness. The new Massachusetts State House was at once acclaimed as a masterpiece, not only by the proud citizens of Boston but by visitors as well, and so it was. When Bulfinch left Boston for Washington to complete the design of the Capitol, Mayor Josiah Quincy expressed the widespread feeling of his contemporaries: "Few men deserve to be held by the citizens of Boston in more grateful remembrance than Charles Bulfinch." He left a lasting mark upon the buildings and topography of Boston.

Elevation and plan of the principal story of the New State House in Boston, by Charles Bulfinch, probably 1797.
THE NEW YORK PUBLIC LIBRARY. ASTOR, LENOX AND TILDEN FOUNDATIONS

Unique in New England is Gore Place in Waltham, Massachusetts, built by the Federalist Governor Christopher Gore in 1805–06. With its spreading symmetrical plan and attached dependencies and its hip roof and tall chimneys, its image is closer to a Southern plantation house than a New England country residence. But in its stately sweep, clean surfaces, elegant proportions, and precise detailing Gore Place is totally Adamesque and very English. The front façade is quite plain, but on the rear the rectangle of the central block is broken by a graceful elliptical bow created by the magnificent oval room that overlooks the broad lawn sweeping down to the river. Gore Place may be, like so many other New England houses, a compendium of ideas, but in this case they were fused into a masterpiece of the Federal style. Its graceful spiral staircase, with simple fragile banisters and sweeping handrail, seems almost to float in air as it soars up the curving wall of the side hall, a gem of elegant simplicity.

Bulfinch's influence in New England was pervasive, especially in Boston, but in other regions throughout the settled and expanding portions of the country, the Federal style was disseminated through the design books by Asher Benjamin. His *The Country Builder's Assistant* (1797) and *The American Builder's Companion; or, A New System of Architecture* (1806) were widely followed by local carpenters in delineating the Federal style, and Greek Revival orders in later editions, with a vernacular or provincial accent in small towns and rural regions throughout New England and the new states in the old Northwest Territories. Certain house types, certain door motifs, certain ornamental details would appear repeatedly over a wide range of the American scene in a persistent bookish manner reminiscent of the stereotypes that left their mark on the architecture of the colonial years.

Decorative Arts in New England

Sweeping changes in New England cabinetmaking and furniture styles closely parallel the transformation of thirteen colonies into a modern nation. With society, economy, culture, and political life in a state of flux, it was no coincidence that cabinetmaking also underwent a sea change in style and shop structure. The new nation was receptive to new ideas after the adoption of the Federal Constitution in 1788. Chippendale furniture had become old-fashioned in London, still the source of fashionable taste for America. The Scottish clergyman Archibald Alison, in his *Essays on the Nature and Principles of Taste* (1790), boldly asserted: "Strong and Massy Furniture is everywhere vulgar and unpleasing. . . . The Taste which now reigns is that of the Antique. Everything we now use, is made in imitation of those models which have been lately discovered in Italy." This revolution in taste was set in motion by a group of adventurous Englishmen with an Arcadian vision who went to Italy and Greece in the 1750s to rediscover the ancient world. James Stuart and Nicholas Revett arrived in Athens in 1751 and published the first volume of *The Antiquities of Athens* in London a decade later; their text and engraved plates of classical ruins were the basis of a new and stimulating architectural style. In 1757 an expedition under Robert Adam set out for the Dalmatian Coast to collect material on the great palace of Diocletian at Spalato. The first volume of his famous *The Works in Architecture* was published in 1773; this and later publications by Adam and his brother, provided authoritative and exciting new visual material on classical architecture and ornament, which had a profound impact on every art and craft in England and America after the Revolution. Although old forms lingered on, new patterns appeared every year thereafter in the London cabinet shops. Although to the public the styles were anonymous, they were summarized and illustrated in *Cabinet-Makers' London Book of Prices* and George Hepplewhite's *The Cabinet-Maker and Upholsterer's Guide*, both published in 1788. Thomas Sheraton's *The Cabinet-Maker and Upholsterer's Drawing Book* (1791–94) and George Smith's *Collection of Designs for Household Furniture and Interior Decoration* (1808) provided cabinetmakers outside of London with reports of the current fashions. As a result of these publications, which were used widely in America, the name Hepplewhite has often been applied to the delicate inlaid and carved furniture with essentially linear forms and square tapering legs, and the name Sheraton has been used to designate furniture employing turned or reeded supports and frequently with bowed (elliptical) or hollowed façades. However, because there is considerable overlap between the styles associated with these two men, in America the term "Federal style" is preferable.

The Federal style in Boston furniture, from about 1790 to 1805, is marked by such attributes as delicate proportions, square tapered legs, patterned stringing and inlays, and sometimes carving. The square-back chair, turned legs, reeded motifs, and certain other carved elements introduced about 1800 were popular until about 1815. The late Federal style, from 1815 onward, was increasingly heavy and bold, marked by marble-top tables and columnar supports, and is called the Empire style.

Detail of a marble-top, tambour-front serving stand probably made in the workshop of Thomas Seymour, Boston, 1805–15, now at Chipstone, Fox Point, Wisconsin. This piece reveals the unusual skill in integrating design and execution and restrained patterns of inlay within the overall concept that is typical of Seymour's cabinetwork. The most striking feature is the veneering of the tambour doors, in which flat strips of dark-stained wood alternate with light strips of birch, with cherry stringing between. The high quality of this piece brings to mind Robert Adam's comment that "the eating rooms are considered as the apartments of conversation . . . it is desirable to have them fitted up with elegance and splendor."

The names of John and Thomas Seymour, father and son, are as inseparably associated with Boston Federal furniture as Bulfinch is with its architecture. Born in England, they emigrated to Portland, Maine, in 1785 and moved to Boston in 1794. They are known to have made furniture for the house Samuel McIntire built in Salem for Elias Hasket Derby, New England's first millionaire, a building described by a visitor from Baltimore "more like a palace than the dwelling of an American merchant." The Seymours are famous for their tambour desks, with sliding tambour doors, or shutters, inlaid with bellflower swags, and with cases veneered with strings of satinwood and drawers fitted with oval bone key escutcheons. Recently furniture historians have questioned the attribution of so much Boston Federal furniture to the Seymours alone. The documented Seymour demilune commode made for Elizabeth Derby, daughter of Elias, was a collaboration of several craftsmen. The case was built in the shop of Thomas Seymour, reeded posts carved by Thomas Whitman, and the still life painted by John Penniman. There were dozens of skilled cabinetmakers working in Boston during the Federal period, and new trends and shop methods of piece work developed, carried on in independent shops frequently located near one another, that increased the exchange of furniture parts and encouraged communal work.

The Dinner Party, by Henry Sargent.
MUSEUM OF FINE ARTS, BOSTON

The Federal furniture of New England was as distinctively regional as its architecture. The primary wood used in the coastal towns was mahogany; cherry was used in the Connecticut River Valley and western Massachusetts, while birch and maple were the preferred woods of northern New England. White pine was the secondary wood throughout the region with the addition of chestnut and tulip in Rhode Island and tulip in Connecticut. Much inlay, lines of light and dark wood known as stringing or banding, was used on Boston pieces, often in geometric patterns. One John Dewhurst is even listed in the Boston Directory for 1809 as "banding and stringing maker." Most Salem chairs, however, have considerable fine carving and little or no inlay. New England chairs usually have stretchers, bracing square tapered legs, although one occasionally sees a Boston chair with reeded legs. Seat frames are squarish, broader in front than in back and sometimes serpentine in front, and upholstered over the seat rail, strengthened at the inner corners with open braces. Pedestal-back and vase-back chairs were common in Rhode Island and Connecticut; this design for modified square-back chairs with stiles bulging outward to meet a serpentine cresting rail can be found in the 1802 edition of *The London Chair-Makers' and Carvers' Book of Prices*. Portsmouth, New Hampshire, and northern New England produced square-back chairs with carved flowers at the corners of the back and with reeded stiles and banisters. The export of furniture to the other ports, particularly in the South, is well documented. The beginnings of the Industrial Revolution were present in the cabinetmaking trade at the end of the eighteenth century in the mass production of Windsor chairs throughout New England, as well as in the chairs manufactured by Lambert Hitchcock in Connecticut and the varieties of so-called "Sheraton fancy chairs" made northward.

As early as 1792, the term "bureau" was used to describe a four-drawer chest; a chest of drawers with a secretary drawer at the top is known today as a "butler's desk" or "escritoire." A "gentleman's secretary" desk and bookcase is usually known as a Salem secretary after its place of origin, while the feminine furniture form of a "lady's cabinet and writing table" are more common to Baltimore. New England bureaus often have serpentine, round, and elliptical fronts, and even the reverse serpentine front, often called ox-bow today after the shape of the yoke, is not an uncommon form. During the Federal period in Massachusetts, it became a practice to fasten a large dressing glass with drawers to the top of a long-legged bureau. Several pieces of this kind have been attributed to Nathaniel Appleton of Salem and to John Seymour and Son in Boston. The rounded drawer fronts with the elliptical sweep are often veneered with figured birch in the urban centers, while in northeastern Massachusetts and New Hampshire oval and rectangular panels of figured birch set in mitered frames of mahogany, sometimes with a dropped panel or tablet in the skirt, were characteristic of the best cabinetwork of the region. Much patterned stringing on the façade and cock-beading for finishing and protecting the edges of the drawers was found on New England case pieces.

Card games—like whist, loo, faro, quadrille, and many others—were highly popular. Many variants of card tables—square, serpentine, and elliptical (bowed)—decorated with inlay, veneers, and carved ornament were made in New England. Card tables, frequently made in pairs, were used as pier or side tables, standing against the wall when not in use. The figured-birch oval veneer within a mitered rosewood or mahogany panel in the skirt was a popular motif in New England. On many of these New England card tables, the serpentine front was modified by an ovolo corner shaped to conform with the projection of the upper part of the turned front legs. In Salem, turned and reeded legs were often used in place of tapered legs on pieces with serpentine ends, elliptical fronts, and ovolo corners. Many of these New England card tables have a feeling of "legginess" and attenuation of form reminiscent of the region's architecture. In architecture and the decorative arts the Federal style in New England is marked by practical ingenuity and refined elegance, severe geometric purity and austere simplicity of thinly proportioned parts.

An Era of Paradox

The Federalist elite envisioned a strong consolidated and commercial empire, led by an energetic government composed of the best, most heroic men in society in place of the impotent confederation of disparate states that unruly popular elements had been allowed to dominate. They believed in leadership by "natural aristocrats," gentlemen who took their political superiority for granted as an inevitable consequence of their social and economic superiority. They were prepared to grant substantial power to the federal government, including the right to tax, regulate commerce, and execute federal laws in order to promote the commercial prosperity of the United States. In effect the Federalists sought to curb the excesses and populist forces the

Revolution had released and to reverse the egalitarian thrust of the turbulent Revolutionary movement. Clinging to an orthodox view of an eighteenth-century hierarchical world of deference and discipline, the Federalist leaders believed that the federal government needed to manipulate the economic forces and harness the self-interest of individuals of the country. Many felt that a cohesive militia and a strong regular army was necessary for the government to meet all external and internal crises. Federalist ideology was rooted in the convergence of classical republicanism and the orthodox language of national covenant: both predicted the collapse of the collective welfare of the people with the spread of individual vice; both promised a broad prosperity upon the achievement of individual virtue. In its classical balancing of the individual and collectivity, Federalism was a hierarchical version of the ancient Harringtonian equation of personal independence and public obligation. And here lay the paradoxical roots of independence in commonwealth deeply embedded in the political culture of New England's orthodox Federalists.

The Federalist reshaping of the social landscape was interwoven with reshaping of the physical landscape. Reports of squalor, ignorance, and violence in the new western settlements of New England deeply disturbed the eastern gentry and revived the old colonial fears of relapse into savagery in the New World. Was civilization moving west, they wondered, or unraveling at the edges? In a series of essays on improvement, the Reverend Nathan Fiske of South Brookfield, Massachusetts, harangued in 1801 against the "slovenliness" of Connecticut River towns; farmers were to "trim and adorn the earth," to drain bogs and swamps, to build "regular and handsome" fencing, and generally to "pay more attention to some things for sake of ornament and sightliness, as well as convenience and advantage." This concern for "ornament and sightliness," as well as for regularity and symmetry was soon to be expressed in the region's architecture through the architectural handbooks of Asher Benjamin, which were important in disseminating the Federal style into the American hinterland. During Timothy Dwight's New England tour, he expressed a typical conservative reaction of the orthodox Federalists to the constant dispersion of the American population along the frontier. Dwight's rambling surveys (posthumously published as *Travels in New England and New York* in four volumes, 1821–22) take in politics, agriculture, scenery, social conditions, and interesting local stories, but above all, they are a celebration of the civilization of compact New England towns of neat clapboard farmhouses, prim village green, and soaring steeple—a civilization based on stability and moderation. Communities of this kind needed time to grow and mature, and they needed their children to remain and sustain them. Rootedness was important in the bonds of community. But emigration to the West that had begun in the 1780s clearly accelerated significantly in the 1790s with an exodus from New England farms to a multitude of new communities spread out across the nation. Loosed from this discipline in the sparsely settled areas of the West, it was too easy for men to revert to savagery, especially since, Dwight was convinced, the frontier was peopled by the dropouts of "regular society," who were unwilling to pay the price of civilization in terms of laws and taxes.

New England was settled by God-fearing Protestants—men and women conditioned by a stern uncompromising Puritan religion. "God sifted a whole Nation that he might send Choice Grain over into this Wilderness," as one of the "elect" put it in 1670. By 1776 they were politically bold beyond any other people, and some of the shared traits of radical Whig ideology and American Puritanism created the idea of a single chosen people destined for a single mission. Yet, random generalizations about this stronghold of conservatism and hotbed of radicalism, of genteel Brahmins and proud immigrants, tend to distort its complex character. New England is a place of contradictory tendencies: here even the climate obviously approves the contention of the ancients that there is dignity in extremes, whereas in half-measures there is nothing but mediocrity and meanness. There the extremes of Federalism and Republicanism, of idealism and despair, of conviction and ambivalence were all represented in the thinking of these shapers of American culture; but even in the diversity of their moods they shared the belief that a new day in human history had dawned.

Gore Place, Waltham, Massachusetts, built in 1805–06 for Christopher Gore, a prominent Federalist figure in the history of the Commonwealth of Massachusetts. There is little evidence on which to attribute Gore Place to any one architect, but while serving in a diplomatic post abroad in 1801, the Gores did meet Jacques Guillaume Legrand, a leading Parisian architect of houses and *hôtels* in the neoclassical style, and he may have acted as a professional consultant in the design. Gore Place is strung along an east–west axis for more than 170 feet on the crest of a gentle southerly slope. A large central two-story block of refined simplicity and harmony dominates; flanking it are narrow connecting wings that terminate in rectangular end pavilions with pedimented gables. In 1809 Edward Augustus Kendall wrote in his travel account through New England: "Mr. Gore's, built and fitted up in patrician style, is the most elegant mansion in New England. It is of *red brick*, a rare circumstance out of the cities and villages, other gentlemen's houses being generally of wood and painted white."

Spiral staircase from the upper landing at Gore Place. The public entrance, with its three-story staircase and twenty-five-foot ceiling, was designed to impress visitors. The floor is King of Prussia marble; the stairs are painted to simulate marble; and the reproduction wallpaper is similar to the "plain stone-colored paper with borders to match" Gore ordered from France. Simplicity and elegance characterize the interiors with the elliptical curves of the of the walls and the decorative restraint of the simple moldings and chair rails. The sweeping flow from room to room, where many large sash windows flood the house with light, gives Gore Place its distinctive character.

Dining room of Gore Place. Adjoining the main public entrance is the state reception hall, a room for banquets, receptions, and balls. The gilt-bronze French Empire chandelier of about 1825 was once owned by Daniel Webster, Gore's law clerk and friend. The covered mahogany, drop-leaf, gateleg table was made in Boston after 1805 and belonged to Gore. The Boston Empire klismos-style chairs were made in Boston about 1820. Robert Roberts, chief butler to the Gores, refers to serving dinner for thirty here every Sunday. The gilded-gesso looking glass, of about 1825, is one of a pair hanging over matching fireplaces at the ends of the room.

Custom House, near Derby Wharf, Salem, Massachusetts, built in 1819 and used until 1937. The Custom House was the focus of Salem's waterfront. Active and retired captains and merchants gathered here for business and gossip; twenty-four employees registered, inspected, and assessed one vessel a day on average. On the first floor, the Surveyor's office was the main room where business was transacted, and where there was a fire-proof vault for records. The Collector and Naval Officer had offices upstairs, with access to the cupola, which gave a commanding view of the harbor. When Nathaniel Hawthorne faced lean times in 1846, his political friends procured for him the position of Customs Surveyor. Salem's commerce had declined by then, and his duties were few. Soon after he lost his position in 1849, he wrote *The Scarlet Letter*. In the introductory essay, "The Custom House," he admitted that his officers, mostly former seamen, spent "a good deal of time . . . asleep in their accustomed corners . . . or boring one another with the several thousandth repetition of old sea stories."

Overleaf

Interior of the First Parish Church, Duxbury, Massachusetts, built in 1840. In the late 1830s Duxbury was riding on a high tide of prosperity, and it seemed appropriate to Weston and others that the First Parish should have a meetinghouse built on a similarly grand scale. Although the third meetinghouse was less than sixty years old, the parish voted to tear it down, and the fourth meetinghouse, the largest in Plymouth County, was erected in its place by Duxbury's skilled ships' carpenters. The design called for an open auditorium eighty-six by sixty-six feet, seating one thousand, with walls more than thirty feet high. The resulting interior, unbroken by columns and with tall windows, creates an atmosphere of extraordinary serenity.

Pews in the First Parish Church. The undulating pattern of mahogany scrolls of the pews is said to represent the waves of the sea. The steeple of the imposing Greek Revival church, which rises to about 127 feet, has served as a landmark for mariners for generations.

The King Caesar House in Duxbury, Massachusetts, built for Ezra Weston, Jr., and his wife in 1808–09. Sturdily built by ships' carpenters, the so-called captain's houses of coastal New England towns reflected the new Federal style design elements introduced to builders by Charles Bulfinch and Asher Benjamin. The house has generous, graceful proportions with a shallow-pitched hipped roof, four tall end chimneys, and brick ends, which are a local feature. Built on Powder Point, the King Caesar House was an appropriate residence for Duxbury's leading shipping magnate. His father became the richest man in Plymouth County, which earned him the nickname "King Caesar"; the son became the second King Caesar.

43

West parlor of the King Caesar House. The window seat overlooks Duxbury Bay. The French scenic wallpaper in this room is *Le Parc Français*, produced in Paris in 1814. The mahogany tall-case clock is typical of examples made in Roxbury around 1800.

Opposite

Central Hall of the King Caesar House. The elliptical fanlight and delicately traced sidelights are original Federal features, and the dado and the cornice were carved by ships' carpenters. Ezra Weston was famous worldwide for his fleet of fine, Duxbury-built ships and for his Boston-based cargo trade that earned him the title of "King Caesar." Weston's house was built to face the wharf on the Bluefish River, but it now overlooks his property on the north bank of the river, today called the Hermon Carey Bumpus Memorial Park.

West parlor of the King Caesar House. The French scenic wallpaper and the elegant Federal details of the woodwork reflect the prosperity and taste that fishing, shipbuilding, and shipping industries brought to the town, particularly to the Westons, who were easily the largest ship-owners of their time in the United States. Weston-grown timber, hauled by Weston oxen, was formed into hulls and spars at Weston shipyards. A Weston mill produced sailcloth, to be cut and sewn at the Weston sail loft. Weston ships brought Manila hemp and iron from abroad to Duxbury to be made by Weston enterprises into rope, tools, fittings, and anchors. Weston farms provisioned the ships, while quantities of salt, imported by the Westons, preserved the fish caught on Weston schooners, which was then exported as cargo.

Overleaf

Dining room of the King Caesar House. The Westons enlarged the room in 1840, at which time they added the marble fireplace surround and the molded cameos in the molding above it. Above the fireplace hangs a Chinese painting of a clipper ship built by Donald McKay in East Boston. The mahogany sideboard was probably made in Boston around 1800, and the girandole looking glass above it is probably European-made, 1805–25.

47

Overleaf

Bedroom in the King Caesar House. The bed curtains and window curtains are *toile de Nantes,* made about 1820, decorated with various historical and biblical scenes. The elaborate pagoda-shaped tea chest was brought home from Asia by a Duxbury ship captain around 1860. Above the mantel hangs a portrait of Priscilla Virgin Weston.

View of the entry hall into the parlor of the Captain Gershom Bradford House, Duxbury, Massachusetts. The house is furnished with Bradford family possessions, many acquired on voyages to Europe and the Mediterranean. As Bradford's great-grandson, also Gershom Bradford, later wrote, "Many a deepwater shipmaster belonged to the First Parish Church. Their womenfolks came to church arrayed in fabrics and adorned with elegancies from the choicest markets of overseas trade. . . . Its members were, perhaps, more familiar with Canton, Honolulu, and the Mediterranean than with Springfield or Albany."

52

Sophia A. Hawthorne

Man's accidents are GOD's purposes

Sophia A. Hawthorne   1843

Nath'l Hawthorne

This is his study

1843

The smallest twig
Leans clear against the sky.

{ Composed by my wife,
and written with her diamond

Inscribed by my
husband at sunset
April 3d 1843

On the gold light ——
            SAH

EK

Opposite
North window of Nathaniel Hawthorne's study at the Old Manse, Concord, Massachusetts. Hawthorne and his wife, Sophia, scratched the inscriptions on the pane at center right: "Man's accidents are God's purposes / Sophia A. Hawthorne 1843"; "Nathl Hawthorne / This is his study / 1843"; and "The smallest twig / Leans clear against the sky. / Composed by my wife, / and written with her dia- / mond / Inscribed by my / husband at sunset / April 3d 1843 / On the gold light—SAH / Sund."

Hawthorne bedroom at the Old Manse. The Old Manse was built as a parsonage by the Reverend William Emerson in 1769–70, and its later notable inhabitant, Nathaniel Hawthorne, made this charming house forever famous in his *Mosses from an Old Manse.* The Hawthornes came to live in the Old Manse in 1842 and chose this front room on the second floor for their bedroom. They gave it a fresh coat of paint and wallpaper and referred to it thereafter as the "golden" room. "Among the houses of Concord," wrote Franklin Sanborn in 1909, a friend and biographer of many of New England's greatest writers, "the Old Manse has had the most romantic history."

The Captain Joshua H. Snow cottage, Edgartown, Martha's Vineyard, Massachusetts, built about 1848. The house exemplifies Edgartown's architectural homogeneity; except for its classical trim and its two chimneys, it is not fundamentally different from houses built a hundred years earlier. The French author and statesman Crèvecoeur remarked in 1782 that the Vineyard "is become a great nursery which supplies with pilots and seamen the numerous coasters with which this extended part of America abounds." In the 1790s New England whalers began exploring the Pacific, and by the 1820s they were pursuing whales to the Hawaiian Islands, Polynesia, Samoa, the Philippines, and the sacrosanct shores of Japan. In subsequent decades they penetrated the frozen vastness of both the Arctic and the Antarctic.

Opposite
The Old Whaling Church (former Methodist Church), Edgartown, Martha's Vineyard, designed by Frederick Baylies, Jr., built between 1843 and 1849. Baylies was Edgartown's most accomplished architect and developed an idiosyncratic neoclassical vocabulary in the fashionable Greek Revival mode in this monumental edifice.

The sanctuary of the Old Whaling Church. The capacious church seats eight hundred in its box pews, once occupied by the whaling captains and their families. The pressed-tin ceiling dates from the late nineteenth century. The Simmons and Fisher organ from Boston was installed in 1869 in a stylish Greek Revival case. Edgartown produced both mariners and builders, and the builders took as much pride in their craft as the seamen did in their more adventurous pursuits of the sperm whale.

The William Vincent (or Vinson) House, Edgartown, Martha's Vineyard, Massachusetts, a one-story, five-bay cottage with a center chimney constructed of early, outsized bricks, built in the late seventeenth century; moved from a cove of Great Pond into Edgartown in 1977. Native pitch pine and oak were used in the post-and-beam framing; the exterior was sheathed with sawn and beveled white pine boards imported from the mainland, but this early siding is now covered with shingles. Of the two front rooms, one has raised paneling of the seventeenth or early eighteenth century while the other was redecorated in the late eighteenth century with a Federal-style mantel and a single-board wainscot with chair rail. Although the Vincent House is an amalgam of periods and styles, it has preserved its integrity as a plain, sturdy dwelling of a New England whaler.

The Dr. Daniel Fisher House, Edgartown, Martha's Vineyard, Massachusetts, built about 1840. Although Edgartown was a thriving community in the early nineteenth century, it is the houses and churches built between 1825 and 1850 in the heyday of whaling that give the village its architectural distinction. During this quarter of a century whaling and such ancillary industries as candle works, sail lofts, ropewalks, and oil manufactures bestowed an unprecedented prosperity on the island. Dr. Daniel Fisher, a physician by profession, came to the Vineyard in 1824. The founder of the first bank on the island and owner of the largest whale-oil works in the world, Fisher was the wealthiest and most influential resident. He built a grandiose house with an elegant, one-story portico supported by two Corinthian columns, with a decorative parapet above with fretwork panels and an octagonal monitor.

Parlor mantel in the Governor John Langdon Mansion Memorial, Portsmouth, New Hampshire, built for Langdon by Daniel Hart and Michael Whidden III, skillful local joiners, in 1783–85. Langdon, as Portsmouth's leading citizen, began construction of an appropriate residence in 1783, building a traditional Georgian structure of imposing design, with some of the finest carved rococo ornament in any American interior. He could have selected Federal motifs to embellish his fireplace walls, as his brother Woodbury Langdon did for his house in 1785, but instead he chose the less fashionable and more conservative, but nonetheless impressive, rococo ornament found in Portsmouth houses erected before the Revolution. The carver copied certain details from the mantelpiece patterns in Abraham Swan's *British Architect*, published in London some forty years earlier.

Opposite

Withdrawing room on the second floor of the first Harrison Gray Otis House, Boston, designed by Charles Bulfinch and built in 1795 and 1796. Otis was the prototypical entrepreneur; he built on his real-estate holdings in what was the then called West Boston, where his first house is situated. He subsequently made a fortune developing Beacon Hill, where Bulfinch designed two further houses for him. This is the most elegant room in the house, embellished with mirrored mahogany doors and elaborate wallpaper. The English japanned fancy chairs belonged to Otis. The musical instruments reflect his accomplishments as an amateur composer.

60

Parlor of the first Harrison Gray Otis House. Otis sold this house on Cambridge Street to John Osborn, a wealthy paint merchant, when he commissioned Bulfinch to build him a second house on Mt. Vernon Street in 1800. The original mantel, with its exceptionally fine neoclassical details, has recently been restored to its original appearance. The huge Boston Federal looking glass of about 1805 resembles one listed in Osborn's 1819 inventory.

Opposite

Façade of the Windsor House, attributed to Asher Benjamin. Built in 1801 for Jonathan Hatch Hubbard in Windsor, Vermont; moved to its present location in southern Connecticut in 1936. In designing the entrance façade, Benjamin applied neoclassical ornament to a typical New England mansion house plan to convey the effect that was both boldly new and traditionally monumental.

Overleaf

Parlor of the Windsor House. Windsor was one of the fastest growing towns in New England at the time this house was built. Located near the head of navigation of the Connecticut River and along a powerful mill stream, it was a distribution center for agricultural produce and an attractive site for water-powered industry in the upper valley. The banjo clock on the wall and the mahogany tall-case clock in the corner were both made by Aaron Willard of Roxbury, Massachusetts, New England's most prolific clockmaker during the Federal period.

Entry hall of the Windsor House. Oval or spiral stairs were among the Federal elements characteristic of Benjamin's innovative style, and he was the first New England builder to perfect their construction. Vertical slats and moldings on the right wall of the staircase echo the oval cherry stair rail and square balusters. The monumental gilded looking glass has a reversed-painted glass tablet depicting Mount Vernon; it was made in New York City about 1800 and was originally owned by the Berenwyck family of Albany. The mahogany tall-case clock was made by Martin Cheney, the leading clockmaker in Windsor, whose name is inscribed on the dial.

Parlor of the Windsor House. The parlor has a number of
similarities to the Federal parlor from the house of Oliver
Phelps to which Benjamin built an addition in 1794 and
1795. The house originally stood in Suffield, Connecticut,
and the parlor is now at Winterthur. Both rooms have
exposed, carved corner columns, richly embellished
cornices, and a chimney breast loaded with cast-plaster
festoons, cornucopias, and classical deities.

Second-floor bedroom in the Windsor House. The design of Jonathan Hubbard's house called for second-floor bedrooms far less ornate than the rooms below, and, therefore, handsomely molded cornices and architraves are the only evidence of the neoclassical style. The mahogany tall-post bedstead was made in New England, 1810–20, and is extravagantly carved, fluted, and inlaid.

Overleaf

The south parlor of the Deshon-Allyn House. The flanking mahogany armchairs and the side chair in the style of Duncan Phyfe are thought to be the work of the reproduction-artist Ernest Hagen of New York City in the 1870s. The Grecian sofa, with gold and black painted decoration, was made in England about 1810. Over the mantel is a portrait of Charles M. Chase of Vermont by Alonzo Slafter and dated 1842; in the corner is a marble bust of Thomas Williams, a Connecticut jurist, modeled by Chauncey B. Ives in Rome, about 1853. The mahogany marble-top pier table was made in Providence, Rhode Island, about 1830; on it is an American whale-oil lamp of about 1840, and above it hangs a gilded American looking glass of the same date.

View through the north parlor window in the Deshon-Allyn House, New London, Connecticut, built of local granite in 1829 by Daniel Deshon, a prosperous merchant, when New London was a major whaling port. The mahogany and mahogany veneer desk-and-bookcase was made in New York City and is attributed to Joseph Meeks and Sons because it is similar to one shown in the firm's famous advertisement of 1833. The marble-top rosewood center table of about 1830 was made in either Manhattan or Brooklyn; it has brass inlay, ormolu mounts, and painted decoration on the pedestal. The transfer-printed Spode tea service dates from around 1820. Flanking the center table are two side chairs from a set of six attributed to John French, who worked in New York City before moving to New London. In the background is a mahogany reclining "Voltaire" library chair, which was made in France during the 1840s.

The north parlor or music room of the Deshon-Allyn House. The mahogany veneered pianoforte was made by William Geib of New York between 1828 and 1838. The harp was made in London in 1831 by Sébastien Erard, and the music stand with brass candle brackets is also English, about 1835. The gilded looking glass is American, made about 1840. David Deshon married Fanny Thurston of Rhode Island in 1826 and built this house in 1829. After Fanny Deshon died in 1833, the house was put up for sale. Unaccountably, seventeen years passed before the property found a buyer—Lyman Allyn, a prominent New London whaling captain who had once been employed by the Deshons. The last of Allyn's children, Harriet, died in 1926, providing in her will for the establishment of the Lyman Allyn Museum, which was built on the campus of Connecticut College between 1930 and 1932.

The second-floor library of the Deshon-Allyn House.
Dominated by a twentieth-century map of Paris, the room is
furnished with a suite of French mahogany furniture of about
1820, which has carved swan's heads for arm supports and is
upholstered with reproduction period fabrics by
Scalamandré. The mahogany and mahogany-veneer
worktable at the right of the sofa is attributed to Duncan
Phyfe's workshop in New York City. The French mahogany
and mahogany-veneer bookcase, adorned with gilt-bronze
sphinx heads and palmettes, dates from about 1830. The
painting above it by Jivan Houtum, 1830, depicts
Mesolóngion, Greece, where Lord Byron died in 1824.

76

The dining room of the Deshon-Allyn House. The dining table, with its elaborately carved pedestals and legs, was made in New York about 1840. It is set with a *vieux Paris* porcelain dessert service of about 1810; on the American mahogany-veneered sideboard of about 1825, decorated with ormolu mounts and hardware, are Sèvres porcelain pieces. Above the sideboard is an English girandole of about 1815. The portrait of Captain John Bolles over the mantel was painted by Isaac Sheffield of New London in 1840.

Dining room in the Barrett House, New Ipswich, New Hampshire, built about 1800 for Charles Barrett, Jr. The design of the house may have been adapted from William Pain's *Guide to House Building,* first published in America in 1796. Barrett graduated from Dartmouth College with a law degree in 1794, married in 1800, and became a well-established businessman in the community. The house was occupied by several generations of Barretts, and its furnishings span the range of time and interests represented by the family. Taken together, they portray a prominent family's history in rural New England.

Opposite
Village of Washington, New Hampshire, which in December 1776 became the first incorporated town named for General George Washington, commander in chief of the Continental Army. This upland wilderness of rocky, infertile soil, and inclement winters in southwestern New Hampshire was settled by pioneer families from Massachusetts. By 1825 the town of Washington had achieved a distinctive look: the authoritative clapboard meetinghouse and the Faxon house commanded the common, and plain, two-story houses were set in a landscape of precipitous hills forested with maple, birch, spruce, hemlock, and pine.

The Faxon House, on the common in Washington, New Hampshire, was built by Azariah Faxon about 1790. The handsome rectangular, seven-bay meetinghouse was raised under the supervision of a Mr. Cummings on the common and finished in 1789; the event was commemorated by a local poet quoting the builder boasting "That every joint he ever framed / He knew would pinch a hair." A year or so after the meetinghouse was completed, Faxon built his elegant, hipped-roof house to the east, also overlooking the common.

Opposite
Doorway of the Johnson House, Woodstock, Vermont, built in 1810.

Ebenezer Alden House, Union, Maine, built between 1797 and 1800. Alden, born in Marlborough, Massachusetts, and a sixth-generation descendant of John and Priscilla Alden of Plymouth, was trained as a carpenter or housewright. He came to Thomaston, Maine, in 1794 with a party of workmen to work on General Henry Knox's grand mansion house, Montpelier, which was completed in 1795. Ebenezer Alden settled in the nearby farming community of Union, purchased land in 1797, and married in 1799, building his house about this time. The floor plan of this pre-Revolution-style house has two well-proportioned front rooms downstairs separated by a hallway and a graceful stair, but the decorative architectural elements—the quoins at the four corners and the handsome pedimented entrance with a fanlight—make the house a charming exemplar of a countryfied but elegant Federal style.

Doorway of the Ebenezer Alden House. This impressive pedimented doorway on the east façade appears to have been based on Plates 38 and 40 in William Pain's *Practical House Carpenter,* which was published in London in 1794 and in Boston in 1796. The mantels in the dining room and parlor are also simplified adaptations of plates from Pain's handbook of designs.

Opposite

Hallway of the Ebenezer Alden House. The ceiling is nine feet, three inches high, and the doorframes are beautifully and delicately carved. The tall-case clock is attributed to Matthew Egerton of New Brunswick, New Jersey, and dates from about 1795. Both the drop-leaf table and the looking glass are from Philadelphia, made about 1760.

The First Baptist Church in Paris Hill, Maine, built in 1838. In 1847, a railroad line was built through Oxford County connecting Montreal, icebound in winter, with the harbor at Portland, Maine, which was open to navigation all year. The railway bypassed Paris Hill because of its elevation, and a new village called South Paris grew up three miles away. Paris Hill had no dependable source of water power so there were none of the gristmills, sawmills, or other industries that brought mercantile prosperity to many New England towns. Hence, the chaste Federal style of its church and houses was rarely changed in the name of improvements, as so often happened in more bustling towns after the Civil War. The clock in the steeple was presented to the town by Hannibal Hamlin in 1883, and the bell was made by Joseph Warren Revere, the son of Paul Revere.

Senate chamber of the State House in Dover, Delaware. The second oldest state capitol in continuous use in the country (after Maryland) and built between 1788 and 1792 (restored 1972–76), the building was occupied by both the State of Delaware and Kent County governments for nearly a century. George Washington's portrait by Denis A. Volozan, commissioned by the General Assembly in 1800 and delivered in 1802, hangs in its original position above the speaker's desk.

*The Expanding National Culture
of the Jeffersonian Republic
in the Middle Atlantic States*

BETWEEN THE EXTREMES of New England and the South, New York and Pennsylvania, as the leaders of the grouping of middle Atlantic states, were distinguished by their "middleness," as Henry Adams put it— their practical and sagacious talent for compromise and the blending of interests. United now with New England, now with Virginia and her southern neighbors, the middle Atlantic states served as a balance wheel, providing the force that in politics and commerce made a nation and in intellectual and artistic activities was ultimately to fuse divergent elements into a national culture.

Philadelphia: The Athens of America

During the middle decades of the eighteenth century, the rapid growth of Philadelphia and its cultural institutions and the tolerance and diversity of its citizens produced a galaxy of talented and learned men unequaled elsewhere in the colonies. In their curiosity about the secular world, their addiction to science, their habit of experimentation, their confidence in reason and improvement, their humanitarianism, and their versatility, they were very much like the European *philosophes*. Under an ever-growing cosmopolitanism, colonial Philadelphia attained preeminence among the cities of early America. Much of the American enlightenment centered on and radiated from Philadelphia, which was indubitably the intellectual center (John Adams called it "the pineal gland") of British America. The founding of the College of Philadelphia in 1740 and the veritable explosion of the number of books owned by Philadelphians epitomized its intellectual growth. When the Englishman Andrew Burnaby traveled through the colonies in 1759 and 1760, he discerned in Philadelphia "some few persons who have discovered a taste for music and painting; and philosophy [science] seems not only to have made a considerable progress already but to be daily gaining ground."

What remarkable men they were, these American *philosophes,* presided over by "the ingenious Doctor Franklin," whose catholic curiosity led him into the fields of public health, heat and ventilation, physics, the theory of medicine, meteorology, geology, chemistry, astronomy, and aeronautics. The American "Age of Reason," as Thomas Paine called it, began with James Logan, a trusted advisor to the Penns, a statesman, and an administrator, who was also the leading botanist in the colony, a student of Newtonian physics, a

92

distinguished classicist, and a patron of artists and scientists of the next generation. There were Thomas Godfrey, who invented an improved mariner's quadrant, and David Rittenhouse, who built the famous orrery and observed the transit of Venus. There were Charles Thomson, secretary to the Continental Congress, an expert in Indian languages, and a classical and Biblical scholar, and William Smith, a product of the University of Aberdeen, who came to America in 1751 and whose visionary book *A General Idea of the College of Mirania* resulted in his appointment as the provost of the College, Academy and Charitable School of Philadelphia. The three men chiefly responsible for the creation of the medical school at the college—John Morgan, William Shippen, and Benjamin Rush—were trained in Edinburgh, and all involved themselves in the struggle for independence and the creation of the new republic. Philadelphia discovered artistic talent in the young Benjamin West, nourished Matthew Pratt, and was the home of the primitive American Museum set up by the Swiss-born Pierre du Simitière.

Acknowledged as the cultural center of colonial America, Philadelphia became its political center. With its strategic location, wealth, learning, industrial and commercial importance, large and cosmopolitan population, and professional and craftsmen classes, Philadelphia was destined to play a crucial role in the American Revolution. In the midst of the war, Pennsylvania adopted a state constitution granting the franchise to almost every male over twenty-one who paid taxes. The colonial merchant upper class lost political leadership and was replaced by radical Whigs, a rising business and professional group that had won approval of the new constitution from the city's skilled artisans and craftsmen. These artisans had assumed that with independence would come freedom from British competition and prosperity, but instead they experienced a severe economic slowdown. Issues such as protective tariff duties for American manufactures, encouragement of trade, and protection of private property were basic to the economic lifeblood of the artisans, a group who did not believe their leaders showed adequate regard for these issues. Such chronic discontents were dismally symptomatic of Philadelphia during the decade of the 1780s. Visitors in 1783 found the city looking as if it had survived a fearful storm: peeling paint and broken windows on houses and shops bespoke years of wartime neglect. The Philadelphia economy, recently forced to redirect itself from maritime commerce to the manufacture of war materials, now had to recover from the dislocations of the war.

In May 1787 Philadelphia staged a grand civic reception for General Washington when he arrived to take his seat in the convention of the states to revise the Articles of Confederation. This convention had been authorized by Congress in answer to pleas for economic assistance from many states. The members of the Constitutional Convention, as the meeting became known, decided their work was so momentous that they quickly chose to exceed their instructions and, holding sessions in complete secrecy, write a new Constitution. Their deliberations persisted through the hot summer and into September. Washington was immediately elected president of the assemblage, and the comings and goings of other prominent men—Edmund Randolph and George Mason of Virginia, Alexander Hamilton of New York, John Rutledge of South Carolina, and many more—revived much of the atmosphere of the 1770s. The citizenry learned little of what was transpiring until the convention adopted a document and the rule of secrecy was repealed. During the signing ceremony on September 17, Franklin announced he was now satisfied that the sun depicted on the back of the president's chair was rising, not setting.

In Philadelphia and throughout Pennsylvania the news that the convention had drawn up a charter for a strong central government sustained the hope that the new frame of government with its larger political arena might rescue the state from much of the destructive factional squabbling and confrontational politics that had plagued it since independence. James Wilson, probably the single most important architect of the new Constitution next to James Madison, led the oratorical battle on behalf of ratification, enthusiastically seconded by Benjamin Rush. The vote in favor of ratification by Pennsylvania was announced to the public on December 12, 1787. When the ninth state—New Hampshire—necessary for the new government to go into operation announced its ratification, the Federalists of Philadelphia decided to celebrate with one of the most spectacular civic observances in the city's history: the Federal Procession on July 4, 1788. The ship *Rising Sun,* anchored in the Delaware River and decorated with the flags of many nations, opened the festivities with a cannon salute at sunrise, echoed by the bells of Christ Church. Ten other vessels flew flags bearing the names of the states that had ratified—Virginia had just followed New Hampshire to make ten. At eight o'clock ten marshals, headed by Thomas Mifflin, wartime quartermaster-general and now a powerful Pennsylvania political leader, led off the parade, followed closely by the Light Horse Troop. Eighty-eight numbered units joined the procession, mainly representing the trades of the city—units thirty through seventy-three in an order determined by lot (32, "Cabinet and Chair-makers"; 40, "Instrument-makers, Turners and Windsor Chair-makers"; 41, "Carvers and Gilders"; and 47, "Upholsterers"). The turnout of the artisans and craftsmen suggests the enthusiasm with which Philadelphia workmen had accepted the Federalist arguments. The mood of reconciliation also permitted replacing the Pennsylvania constitution of 1776, with its single-house legislature unchecked by any other authority, with a state constitution modeled closely on the federal, particularly in separating and balancing the legislative, executive, and judicial powers.

Among the reasons for Philadelphia's hearty support of the Constitution was the hope that a new start in government would bring the national capital back where it belonged—to the largest, wealthiest, and most centrally located city in the Union. The population of the city and the adjacent districts, estimated at 38,798 in 1782 had grown to 42,520 by the first census of 1790. But Philadelphia seemed too wickedly urban to puritanical and backwoods congressmen from New England and the South, despite the claim of the *Federal Gazette* that Philadelphia was filled with "Americans who exhibited the ancient simple Republican manners of our country." A bill setting the permanent site on the Potomac River but naming Philadelphia as the temporary capital failed during the first session of the new Congress. As municipal officials lobbied for the city and Pennsylvania congressmen bargained and dithered to make Philadelphia the permanent capital, Alexander Hamilton sealed his famous pact with Secretary of State Thomas Jefferson to locate the capital on the Potomac River. During the debates the high Federalist Fisher Ames of Massachusetts grumbled about the rival lobbying for Philadelphia and New York as a "despicable grog-shop contest, whether the taverns of New York or Philadelphia shall get the custom of Congress."

At least Philadelphia had the temporary capital, and there were those who thought that once the seat of government was in the city inertia would prevail. Refurbishing since the war had made much of the city attractive again: Penn's town plan was basically intact in the 1790s with its red-brick houses punctuated by the steady rhythm of white casement windows and pedimented doorways facing red-brick pavements lined with buttonwood, willow, and Lombardy poplar trees. Some thought this pleasant orderliness boring; others were impressed with the regularity and neatness. John Cotton, a visitor in 1815, observed: "Philadelphia is an elegant and well-constructed city, vastly superior in external appearance to any we have seen. . . . The streets are very spacious and clean and the sidewalks in every street wide enough for five or six persons to walk abreast, handsomely paved with brick. The streets all cross at right angles and are perfectly straight."

Architectural styles had changed little from the Georgian of the colonial era; plentiful regional materials, such as brick and marble, and local craftsmen trained by apprenticeship guaranteed continuity of style. In 1785 the Pennsylvania Assembly voted to grant the American Philosophical Society a plot of ground within the State House Yard along the west side of Fifth Street; there in 1787 the society erected a relatively unadorned rectangular, symmetrical structure in harmony with the State House. Similarly, the Philadelphia County courthouse built along Chestnut Street just west of the State House in 1787–89 and the City Hall constructed east of the State House in 1790–91 followed traditional red-brick Georgian lines, though the addition of cupolas gave them a slight air of pretension. With the arrival of the federal government, the first of these structures became Congress Hall, accommodating the House of Representatives on the first floor and the Senate on the second, and the City Hall took in the Supreme Court.

In contrast was Library Hall, designed by Dr. William Thornton, a young physician and gentleman-architect recently arrived from the Virgin Islands with no professional qualifications whatsoever. He gave the building a Palladian elegance and delicacy of detail hitherto rarely seen in Philadelphia—with four colossal pilasters and an ornamental balustrade, the whole representing a more literal Palladianism than had ever prevailed before in Philadelphia. Thornton described his method: "I got some books and worked a few days, then gave a plan in the ancient Ionic order which carried the day." When the wealthy merchant William Bingham offered to donate a white marble statue of Franklin for an alcove on the front of the building, the impression of neoclassicism became complete; indeed at Franklin's own suggestion the statue was clothed in a toga.

In 1788–89 William Hamilton, grandson of Andrew Hamilton, one of the builders of the State House, brought the new Federal style to Woodlands, his estate outside Philadelphia. The exterior is one of the earliest examples in America of the classic Palladian block with a monumental freestanding portico in the Doric order, and the interior boasts a rich variety of spaces. A prominently lateral rectangular hall with semicircular ends runs across the main axis behind the portico. To the left and right of the main hall are square rooms; immediately adjacent to and behind the hall on the main axis is a smaller, circular hall; the rooms to the left and right behind are oval with enormous bowed ends. On the exterior of the house, there is no hint of this internal variety in shape, proportion, and orientation. All of this has its counterpart in the interior planning arrangements of Robert Adam and his circle. The introduction of complex curved shapes—the use of the circle and the ellipse—for interior spaces behind a fundamentally conservative Palladian rectangular block with a pedimented central pavilion is characteristic of the Federal style in Philadelphia. Yet, Woodlands does exhibit several exterior features of the emerging Federal style. The Doric columns are tall and thin and the modillioned cornice that crowns the house is delicate in scale. Over the central door is an elliptical fanlight, and Palladian windows to the left and right of the portico are set back slightly in a secondary plane of the wall. The stone house was originally covered with stucco creating a smooth, flat wall surface in which the window openings are sharply defined. The corners of the building are precisely cut, without quoins, and from the side, the walls of the oval rooms are seen to push out in a swelling curve. This tension between curved and rectilinear surfaces is characteristic of Federal architecture.

Bank of Pennsylvania, by Benjamin Henry Latrobe
HISTORICAL SOCIETY OF PENNSYLVANIA

The first public building in Philadelphia to adopt the neoclassical temple façade with freestanding Corinthian columns was a new First Presbyterian Church, built in 1793 on the site of the congregation's earlier church on the south side of Market Street between Second and Third. Next came the Bank of the United States. A federally chartered bank was the centerpiece of Secretary of the Treasury Alexander Hamilton's program to use the Constitution to place the Union's finances on a sound footing and to encourage commerce with the help of governmental authority. The Bank of the United States opened for business in December 1791 in Carpenter's Hall with Thomas Willing as its president. In 1794 the stockholders acquired a lot on the west side of Third Street between Chestnut and Walnut, and construction of a new building was begun in 1795 based on a design by Samuel Blodget, Jr., a New Hampshire-born businessman and amateur architect. Blodget chose the classical grand order of the Greco-Roman temple that has endured as an icon of American banking. Six freestanding Corinthian columns of blue Pennsylvania marble support the pediment and entablature; inside eight Corinthian columns support a balcony and forty small Corinthian columns bear the weight of a low dome with a skylight. The imposing building was worthy of Hamilton's ambitions for the institution—except for one conspicuous cost-cutting change in Blodget's plan. As the architect complained, "the brick sides are an injurious deviation."

In the Federal era Philadelphia reached the peak of its eminence. Until 1800 it was the capital of the new nation, and with its coterie of scientists, artists, and philosophers, it was the intellectual capital as well. Unchallenged in finance, Philadelphia was the home of almost half of all banking capital in America. The city boasted the most extensive and varied industry in the country and a substantial foreign commerce. Philadelphia was also the starting point for much of the western trans-Allegheny trade. To the opening of the frontier the Pennsylvania Germans contributed the Conestoga wagon, an adaptation of the European peasant's wagon, and the Kentucky rifle—a lighter, more accurate weapon with a smaller bore and with rifling to increase its range. Using the Conestoga wagon, with its capacity for two tons of cargo, traders carried furniture, tools, household wares, even printing presses, to the new communities beyond the mountains in return for grain or flour or whiskey. Together with the keelboat in facilitating internal trade, they helped make Philadelphia the largest city in the nation. At the turn of the century, however, Philadelphia was losing its prominence to New York, a bustling, noisy, smelly city packed into the lower tip of Manhattan.

New York: Gateway to the American Rhine

New York's commercial prominence was in part the result of topography. At no other spot on the North Atlantic coast was there such a splendid harbor so favorably situated for the combination of transatlantic, coastal, and inland trade. New York harbor is protected by long stretches of beach upon which the surf pounds incessantly: the outer shore of Long Island, stretching eastward from Coney Island to Montauk Point and the New Jersey coast extending from Sandy Hook to Cape May. This landlocked harbor offered more perfect natural shelter from the surges of stormy seas than that of any other major American port as close to the sea. Like its rivals, New York serviced a large agricultural hinterland. Its initial advantage, however, was the Hudson River. Navigable 150 miles inland to Albany, the Hudson was the first stage in the "water level" route to the West, which was to give New York a marked advantage over the other ports. Commercial agriculture flourished on either side of the river. From Albany, a ribbon of cultivated land ran west along the Mohawk, and to the east and north the farms of New York merged with those of Vermont and touched Quebec at the head of Lake Champlain. Two major roads ran west from the Hudson to a point near Rochester, and by 1800 farmers were pushing into the Genesee Valley and on to the watershed of the Allegheny. All told, transportation and migration were comparatively easy through these farmlands running north and west, and New York City was a natural gateway.

Federal Architecture in New York

The New York City Hall was built in 1811–12 from a design submitted by Joseph-François Mangin and John McComb, Jr., in 1802. It is one of the few French-inspired buildings of the period, perhaps because the horrors of the Reign of Terror dampened an earlier enthusiasm for things French. One of the most monumental buildings of the early Federal style in America, it contains a magnificent central stairway. Available evidence indicates that the original design was Mangin's, while its actual construction as well as the conservative adaptation of its detailing to a more English Adamesque mode, belonged to McComb. Today few eighteenth- and early nineteenth-century landmarks survive in New York, and one must rely on pictorial evidence for the changing visions of urban reality. In anticipation of the city's selection as the capital at the time of Washington's inauguration on April 30, 1789, the old City Hall (Federal Hall) was remodeled by Pierre Charles L'Enfant in 1788–89 with a new wing at the rear to accommodate the national government. A view of Federal Hall at the time of Washington's inauguration was drawn by Peter Lacour, a French painter and designer who visited America after the Revolution, and then engraved on copper by Amos Doolittle of New Haven, who published it in 1790. When the capital was moved to Philadelphia the next year, Federal Hall once again became City Hall with seventeenth-century Dutch gabled buildings among its more picturesque neighbors.

Federal Hall and Wall Street, watercolor by Archibald Robertson, 1798.
THE NEW-YORK HISTORICAL SOCIETY

The new Government House, with a projecting portico supported by four colossal Ionic columns, was erected in 1790 as the residence of the President. When the capital moved, it became the governor's mansion, occupied first by George Clinton and then by John Jay. Then the state capital moved to Albany in 1797, and the handsome structure facing Bowling Green at the foot of Broadway was leased as a boardinghouse. It was subsequently used as the Custom House; it was torn down in 1815 and the present United States Custom

100

House occupies the site. Richmond Hill, a country estate built in 1767 about a mile and a half outside the city (where Charlton and Varick streets now intersect), was occupied by Vice President Adams in 1789–90. An engraving of the house by Cornelius Tiebout was published in the June 1790 issue of *New-York Magazine*. Mount Vernon, or "Smith's Folly" as it was called, was planned and started in 1795 by Colonel William Stephens Smith and his wife, Abigail (daughter of John Adams). Reverses in fortune compelled Smith to sell the place, and it was acquired by William T. Robinson, who completed it in 1798–99. The house, considered one of the finest estates on Manhattan, burned in 1826 and was never rebuilt. But the stone stable building survived and still stands on its original site (now East Sixty-first Street between First and York avenues near the Queensborough Bridge) and serves as the headquarters of the Colonial Dames of America.

There is also a positive footnote from the squandered human potentialities of the Hamilton-Burr duel in 1804: Hamilton's charming country house, The Grange, still stands at Convent Avenue and 141st Street, and the Jumel Mansion at 161st Street overlooking the Harlem River valley, where Burr lived with his second wife, Madame Jumel, are both now house museums. In 1810 Stephen Jumel bought the old summer home of the loyalist Roger Morris, which had served as Washington's headquarters during the Battle of Harlem Heights, and then remodeled it in the neoclassical style. After the Revolution, New York enjoyed a state-wide housing boom. In 1805–06 States Dyckman built Boscobel, an elegant twenty-room mansion that is a model of Federal grace, in Westchester County (later Montrose, New York). In 1961, the house was moved to another Hudson River site in Garrison and formally opened to the public.

The neoclassical Bartow-Pell Mansion in Pelham Bay Park, New York, facing Long Island Sound, was built sometime between 1836 and 1842 for Robert Bartow on land that his ancestor Thomas Pell had bought from the Indians in the seventeenth century. The house had deteriorated considerably when in 1914 the newly formed International Garden Club leased it from the city, had it restored by the firm of Delano and Aldrich, and then opened the house to the public in 1946. While John Bolton, a nephew of the English architect William Jay, is thought to have constructed the mansion, Minard Lafever, a friend of the Bartow family, may have contributed to the design of the house or recommended the use of his builders' guides.

The American Rhine and the Erie Canal

The Hudson River, called the "American Rhine" by admiring foreigners, was one of the nation's major arteries. Farmers in the Hudson Valley were favorably situated to export their wheat, but those further inland found that the cost of dragging a wagon over miserable roads in the summer or by sleigh in the winter ate up the market value of the grain. The most pressing economic problem of the frontier farmer, chained to a life of self-sufficiency, was the transportation and marketing of his products. He could not function as an efficient husbandman, carpenter, woodsman, lumberman, toolmaker, cobbler, and handyman at one and the same time. Providing food, clothing, and tools for the family meant drudgery and poverty relieved only by the hope that better times were coming after the first hardships of settlement had passed. Only if they could find a single crop worth carrying to market could settlers pay for their land, buy such necessities as ironware and salt, and hope for a rising standard of living. The obvious solution was the construction of turnpikes and improvements in waterways that would cut down the cost of transporting goods to market. The back country would be of no use to the port as a consumer of imports unless it could offer something of commercial value with which to purchase them. Flour overshadowed all other lesser offerings. As far back as 1686 when a new state seal was being designed, the flour barrel had been included with the beaverskin as the basis of New York's prosperity, and it had continued to be the principal offering.

In 1815 DeWitt Clinton made a remarkable speech calling for the construction of canals to link the Hudson River with Lake Erie and Lake Champlain. Two years later he pushed through the state legislature an act for the digging of the Erie Canal, which took eight years to complete. Few undertakings have so completely fulfilled the highest claims and fondest hopes of its sponsors as did the Erie Canal. Its amazing success in raising land values, stimulating the growth of cities, and providing easy access to markets converted all but the most skeptical to the importance and desirability of internal improvements in New York State. Wheat brought in the greatest cash returns, and as the center of production moved westward the Genesee Valley won the nickname of "The Granary of America" soon after the Erie Canal reached Rochester in 1823.

The Erie Canal was pushed forward with a vigor and a speed not commonly associated with public enterprise. In October 1825 New York celebrated its completion with a statewide jubilee, as the first boat made the journey from Buffalo to New York, where the city witnessed an impressive ceremony as Governor Clinton poured a keg of Lake Erie water into the ocean. The creation of the Empire State by 1825 was the combined achievement of hundreds of thousands of New Yorkers in scores of occupations. If two groups deserve special mention, they are the pioneer farmers of the hinterland and the various merchants of the port of New York. The former conquered the wilderness and made New York a leading agricultural state; the latter drew to New York the bulk of the transatlantic, coastal, and interior trade of the nation. Central and western New York received the greatest benefits from the canal. Wheat grown in the region west of Utica, formerly turned into whiskey or fed to pigs, could reach tidewater inexpensively, and cities along the Erie Canal became boom towns.

The Rise of Baltimore

In the 1790s Baltimore's population more than doubled, from 13,503 in 1790 to 31,514 in 1800. With its bustling port and hustling shippers, that population increased to 36,000 in 1810 and to 63,000 by 1820. Its tubby freighters carried its tobacco, rye, rye whisky, and wheat down the Patapsco River, bound for lesser coastal towns, or steering through the capes of the Chesapeake Bay outbound for distant harbors. Baltimore lies nearly two hundred miles from the ocean, but it has a salt tide which laves the docks and piers that line its nearly one hundred miles of foreshore. During the late eighteenth century, there were two civilizations in Maryland, one a tobacco plantation civilization to the south, dependent on indentured servants, slaves, and debt and the other based on wheat, grown mostly by pioneers of small means, made up of Englishmen, Germans, Irishmen, Swedes, Bohemians, and a few Frenchmen living to the north and west of Baltimore. Wheat farming did not rely on slave labor or capital supplied by British merchants. In the Federal period this civilization became predominant in Baltimore. At the same time, a third civilization was emerging, a maritime civilization that found its recruits on the Eastern Shore and sprang up wherever the combination of water and timber made shipbuilding possible. The romantic reputation of Baltimore as a port is based upon the phrase "Baltimore clipper"—not a clipper ship with three masts all rigged with square sails but a schooner. In this

103

golden age of sail, she might be rigged as a brig or a brigantine for special purposes. Every tidewater planter had to have a boat, and the building of Chesapeake schooners around the rim of the bay was a major industry, ranking next to agriculture.

The basis of Baltimore's trade in the Federal period was the flour made from the hard wheat of its back country and ground in the mills on its own streams. Its chief market was the West Indies, although there were developing outlets in Spain, Portugal, and the Mediterranean. The typical West Indian schooner leaving Baltimore carried a cargo of flour, barrel staves (for the molasses trade), dried fish (mostly herring and shad), Indian corn (from the Eastern Shore), and dry goods (previously imported from Germany). The West Indian trade was difficult, given French and English blockading, but blockade-running was an old game to Baltimore skippers. After the cargo was sold, the vessel would bring back raw sugar, molasses, coffee, and perhaps lemons and other citrus fruit. This trade was exceedingly profitable, and those engaged in it suddenly found themselves men of vast resources. By November 1790, the legislature granted a charter to a group of citizens to found the Bank of Maryland. In 1796 the merchants, under the pressure of the clergy, put up money to organize what was called the Library Company, a collection of books which would later form the nucleus of the Maryland Historical Society. On December 31, 1796, Baltimore became a legally incorporated city, with all the rights and privileges thereunto pertaining, including the right to lay taxes and spend them within its own borders. Within the space of a single generation, Baltimore Town rose from a wilderness village to a thriving center serving the market needs of a new hinterland area, as the merchants of Baltimore became important figures in the commercial world.

The second half of the eighteenth century had witnessed a sudden take-off for Baltimore: from a mere village of twenty-five wooden houses in 1752, it grew to a brick-and-mortar town of more than 30,000 inhabitants by 1800 and crystallized as the central place of Maryland. Baltimore, situated on the fall line at the junction of piedmont and tidewater, was an offspring of the economic growth of the piedmont, the Delaware, Brandywine, and Susquehanna valleys of the north. Flour mills and iron furnaces were being built in Delaware and Pennsylvania, and a frontier of wheat farming was moving southward, in conjunction with the immigration and settlement of the Germans and the Scotch-Irish. Mill seats began to be established in the Baltimore region, where the "fall" or "run" of streams that ran down from the piedmont provided several hundred feet of head at the "fall line" before it reached tidewater, offering numerous sites for water-driven mills.

During the Revolution, the generation that had founded the town of Baltimore died out, and the young men who rose to power in the army, privateering, and manufacturing constituted a new set of leaders who retained ever after a certain glamor, national idealism, and keen appreciation of risk. As Latrobe explained to Tocqueville years afterward, their daring reinforced their popularity with the people, particularly the artisans and craftsmen in Baltimore, and made it possible for them to retain their elite leadership and decision-making in the period of the new nation. Baltimore became a community of immense self-confidence and creativity, and in the 1790s a knot in the world's web of shipping, finance, and communications in which a large share of the craftsmen were dependent on the commercial sector for patronage. "The most flourishing commercial town on the continent," was the comment of one visitor at the turn of the century. By 1804 there were fifty mills within eighteen miles of the city making flour for shipment, while tobacco continued to be an important article of export. Visitors to Baltimore were impressed with the bustle of shipping and construction and recounted its impressive growth. "Some forty years ago it consisted of several fishermen's huts," wrote Paul Svinin, a Russian traveling in the United States about the time of the War of 1812, in his description of Baltimore. "Now it is one of the fairest cities of North America, in point of wealth and trade, occupying the first place after Philadelphia, New York, and Boston." Population doubled in the two decades after 1800 as it had in the 1790s, and the accumulation of people required an accumulation of houses providing a showcase for the accumulation of wealth.

Baltimoreans determined to build on a scale to exploit its piedmont setting. The original sites for the cathedral and the Washington Monument were abandoned in order to place them upon the crest of a hill. Other new institutions were sited on the west and northwest of the city in this construction boom to obtain the advantages of better drainage, cheaper ground, or because their presence might threaten a densely populated district. Ordinary houses and warehouses were built in rows of six to twelve at a time, and financial pools were created to insure them, since a single fire might destroy a range of dwellings and warehouses. As individual merchants piled up fortunes, they began to display their private wealth in the site and scale of town dwellings designed by architects, while the planter aristocracy built magnificent country houses such as Homewood and Mount Clare. Collective enterprises and new institutions modeled on Philadelphia were incorporated for public uses. In 1809 seventeen hundred persons subscribed $20,000 to the Athenian Society to promote American-made goods.

Cross-sectional drawing of the Baltimore Cathedral, by Benjamin Henry Latrobe.
ARCHIVES OF THE ARCHDIOCESE OF BALTIMORE

Other institutions to support literature, building, mechanics, medicine, agriculture, and science are traceable to this network of gifted and articulate men who began to pool their capital for civic improvement and civic grandeur. Cosmopolitan Baltimore, in its pride, sought a scale and style to rival the old-world cities of culture and history. And buildings would express meanings and impose order. The most impressive domes and steeples to rival one another in lifting out of the mass of houses were the Catholic cathedral, the Exchange, the Unitarian church, Saint Paul's Episcopal Church, First Baptist, and the "superb edifice" of the beautiful domed Medical College. The courthouse, admired as "an immense edifice," was built between 1805 and 1809, and nearby was the Masonic Hall, which later served as a federal courthouse. The search for meaning and the passion for imposing order on this complex cityscape by the citizens of Baltimore in neoclassical public buildings resulted in the presence for a number of years of such remarkable architects as Benjamin Henry Latrobe, Robert Mills, and Maximillian Godefroy. Vital to this network were several editors of

106

considerable persuasive powers, in person as well as in print. One was William Gwynn, publisher of the *Federal Gazette*, backer of a type foundry, and influential in backing the Hibernian Society and the literary circle known as the Delphian Club. Active in the Delphian Club were the authors of three immortal American songs: Francis Scott Key, "The Star Spangled Banner"; John Howard Payne, "Home, Sweet Home"; and Samuel Woodworth, "The Old Oaken Bucket." Another was Fielding Lucas, bookseller of French titles, publisher of fine books, and founder of the Baltimore Harmonic Society, which was central to the musical life and charitable efforts of the city. Through his *Register,* a weekly with national circulation, Hezekiah Niles helped formulate the "American system" of public works and protective tariffs for manufacturing. And John Skinner's *American Farmer*, probably the nation's most important agricultural journal, also reported on technical and medical devices. The merchant city of Baltimore was part of a dynamic circulation system of goods, money, and information. The accumulation of wealth, visible in the new private and public buildings, depended on the flow of money and goods. "Commerce is the main spring of this City," a local physician noted in 1819, as the number of banks increased from two to nine.

At the very peak of its prosperity in the 1820s, Baltimore was faced with a serious threat to its own future growth: it focused on capturing the western trade. The opening of the Erie Canal in 1825, providing an unbroken waterway from the Great Lakes to New York City, had begun to divert valuable western trade which had hitherto gone to the port on the Chesapeake. What was to be done? To meet the crisis, a far-seeing group of Baltimore merchants hit upon the bold scheme of building a railroad all the way to the Ohio River. It seemed a mad enterprise of speculation, for railroads were then in their infancy. But on July 4, 1828, the whole town and hosts of visitors gathered at Mount Clare where, with solemn ceremony, the cornerstone of the Baltimore and Ohio Railroad was laid. Charles Carroll of Carrollton, Baltimore's "Grand Old Man" and the last surviving signer of the Declaration of Independence, then a "relic" at ninety-one, turned the first spade of earth.

The railroad itself was the basis for land speculation in this era of city building; as John Latrobe described it later, each person saw the railroad as "the rose of a vast watering pot" that would irrigate his property.

Baltimore's economy grew more complex and interconnected, and the shape it took in the 1820s defined its structure until the Civil War. Its successes vindicated the "American system" of manufactures promoted so energetically in the early years of the nineteenth century. As projected, commerce and manufacturing were not rival forms of enterprise any more, but woven together. By the late 1820s Baltimore no longer traded primarily in re-exports; far more substantial were the home-processed materials of the region and impressive quantities of local manufactures. The protective tariff had succeeded in nursing new industries that now supplied the American market more cheaply and were beginning to compete in the world market. In one week, 12,000 chairs of Baltimore manufacture were shipped to South America. A new prosperity, a new excitement, a new speculation took hold of Baltimore in the 1820s.

Decorative Arts of Middle Atlantic States

Each of the burgeoning American coastal cities had been born of widely different circumstances; each had been shaped differently by its separate colonial experience; and each developed a regional expression in the decorative arts that, in the generation following the Revolution, is especially recognizable in cabinetwork. Although the designs that were characteristic of each center were based, sometimes quite literally, on English (and to some degree later on French) design books, in different ways they took on obvious American attributes. The rocketing prosperity of Baltimore's thriving commerce attracted many new residents to the port and caused a flurry of building activity. All this prosperity and construction created a large new market for the cabinetmaker's trade, and the 1790s witnessed an influx of skilled craftsmen to the city in furniture-related industries to share in the opportunities created by the city's boom. Some well-to-do Marylanders ordered their furniture directly from London firms, and the impact that the local furniture manufacturers felt from these English imports may explain why the school of design that arose in Maryland was closer to English patterns than that of any other in America. A London fashion gracefully expressed in Baltimore was painted furniture—American "fancy" furniture as it was termed during the period—a fad that supported some fifty-odd makers and painters working in the city at the turn of the century. Among the leading practitioners of the fancy furniture craftsmen were John and Hugh Finlay, Irish born and trained, who advertised as early as 1803

"FANCY and JAPANNED FURNITURE . . . all colors, gilt, ornamented . . . with Flowers, Trophies of Music, War, Husbandry, Love . . . with or without views adjacent to the city." Most painted-furniture makers of the early nineteenth century produced seating furniture; Baltimore estate inventories indicate that middle- and upper-income households often contained several sets of fancy seating furniture and a variety of other forms. Carvers and gilders who made looking glasses and picture frames were another furniture specialization in Baltimore after 1790; since there were many retailers of imported goods, these craftsmen met much competition from British exports. Possibly the most distinctive form of ornamentation expressed on Baltimore Federal furniture was *verre églomisé* of biblical and allegorical figures, a technique of painting glass panels on the reverse with gilded and polychrome decoration, and used to ornament the tablets of looking glasses and as the decorative inserts on desks for ladies. Another specialization within Baltimore cabinetmaking was that of the inlay maker. In Baltimore the bellflower—the "husk and drop" with the elongated central petal—inlaid on table, desk, and chair legs is distinctive as is the "half circular shade" on fan and shell-like ornaments inlaid on table tops and chests of drawers. When Thomas Barrett, a cabinetmaker who specialized in inlaid furniture, died in 1800, his estate inventory showed the large quantities of inlays he made and stocked, included 621 yards of "bands" and 1316 "shells." One of Barrett's successors, William Patterson, clearly listed in the city directories as a cabinetmaker, stated in an 1800 newspaper advertisement that he had "commenced the Manufacturing of Stringing, Banding, and Shells of every description." Mahogany and exotic mahogany veneers were overwhelmingly favored as the primary wood in fine Baltimore Federal furniture; Baltimore cabinetmakers used walnut rarely except in simple pieces and, as in the colonial period, used tulip poplar, white cedar, and white pine (and to a less degree hard yellow pine) as secondary woods for drawer linings. The primarily flat surface decoration of the early Federal era, when the profuse and artful use of inlay with eagles, shells, and floral-and-leaf motifs were the hallmark of this style, gave way after 1815 to three-dimensional embellishment of surfaces. The principal types of ornamentation of Baltimore late Federal and Empire furniture are veneers, turning, reeding, carving, and painting. Veneering was handled differently by the second decade of the nineteenth century: the satinwood banded oval panels in mitred frames were replaced by the rectangular panels of dark mahogany with crossbanding and beading shaped in Gothic arched panels. Turned elements of bold vase and triple-ring turnings were used in the late Federal period on chair and table legs, as were turned tapered freestanding classical columns for supports for tables and sabre legs for chairs. Reeding and carving (acanthus and fruit motifs), along with painted ornamentation (romantic landscapes, stylized anthemions, fruit and shells, vines and leaves, trophies, swans, and winged thunderbolts) painted against a dark ground and rosewood graining are characteristic of Baltimore Empire furniture. In no other American city were English furniture styles and decorative ornaments interpreted with such exuberance.

"Philadelphia may be considered the metropolis of the United States," wrote Jacques Brissot de Warville in 1788. "It is certainly the most beautiful and best-built city in the nation, and also the wealthiest, though not the most ostentatious. Here you find more well-educated men, more knowledge of politics and literature, more political and learned societies than anywhere else in the United States." Philadelphia, at the junction of the Schuylkill and Delaware rivers, was the largest and richest American city in the Federal era and held the shipping supremacy of the United States until about 1797. In the highly sophisticated and wealthy community of Philadelphia of merchants, mariners, and mechanics, there was ample demand for furniture in the latest styles and there were craftsmen who were able and ready to satisfy the most exacting customers.

During the Chippendale era preceding the Revolutionary War, the cabinetmakers of Philadelphia won lasting acclaim with the exuberant, richly carved pieces they fashioned in the rococo style. In the waning years of the eighteenth century, those masters were largely replaced by a new generation of craftsmen who came to work in the largest city in America. As one observer pointed out in 1794, "No cabinetmaker can miss of employment there." That year the first major volume of American cabinetmaking prices for workmanship, entitled *The Philadelphia Cabinet and Chair-Makers' Book of Prices* was published in Philadelphia. The publication of this book by the journeymen marked the beginning of a labor battle between employer and employee that ended in a strike in 1796. Using highly grained maple and satinwood veneer outlined by decorative inlay of stringing and crossbanding against contrasted woods, these cabinetmakers worked out with decorative inlays an endless variety of designs in cabinet and chair furniture. Square-back chairs with carved and reeded spindles were popular in Philadelphia, in which large quarter-round blocks braced the corners. Even in the Federal period many chairs had side rails completely tenoned through the rear legs—commonly called "open tenons" on the

110

back. White painted and gilded furniture was favored by John Adams, Thomas Jefferson, Robert Morris, and other eminent Americans, many of whom had French examples in their homes and all of whom lived in Philadelphia at some point during the years when the city was the national capital. Philadelphia cabinetmakers also relied heavily on string inlay and crossbanding for decorative effect. Chair frames were constructed of ash, white oak, and sometimes walnut, while drawers were made with tulip poplar as the secondary wood. In 1807 Ephraim Haines made a set of black ebony furniture for the French-born financier Stephen Girard, one of Philadelphia's most prominent citizens and the wealthiest man in the United States when he died in 1831. In 1811 Haines went into the lumber business, and a German cabinetmaker, Henry Connelly, took over Girard's patronage. The work of the two craftsmen had much in common: both were indebted to the plates of Thomas Sheraton's *Drawing-Book* for many of their patterns and they probably used the same specialists for turning and carving. During this period in the early nineteenth century, the practice of stocking "ready-made" furniture for retail sale replaced the earlier tradition of "bespoke" work, a special order placed by the client with the cabinetmaker.

Within the thirty years following 1800, this checkerboard city of red-brick houses trimmed in white was transformed into something new—the first major American industrial city. Beset with difficulties and distresses, the people of Philadelphia during this quarter century created the institutions and laid the foundations for the great industrial city that was to come. While doing so, they reached a higher level of intellectual and artistic life than any other city of the United States. Gilbert Stuart, after he moved to Boston from Philadelphia, liked to remember this, and began his anecdotes with "When I resided in the Athens of America." In 1811, Latrobe, while finishing up his Philadelphia commissions and busy with the Capitol and the President's House in Washington, addressed the Society of Artists of the United States, expressing his optimism about progress in Philadelphia and predicted that the ideals represented by the arts of the ancient world would continue, and that "the days of Greece may be revived in the woods of America, and Philadelphia become the Athens of the Western world." On the surface all seemed well with the city; at a testimonial dinner in 1825 Commodore John Barron held forth his glass and declaimed: "Philadelphia—justly acknowledged to be the first in the arts, and second to none in whatever can contribute to the grandeur, respectability, and comfort of a city!" Yet Philadelphia had already lost her rank as the country's largest city and most important trading center.

Historically Philadelphia had prospered as the "bread basket" of the colonies and the young Republic, but the westward shift of population had cost her primacy in the export of flour as the produce of the western part of the state now went down the Susquehanna to Port Deposit, at the head of tidewater navigation, for trans-shipment to Baltimore. Philadelphians were dismayed at how the shipping tonnage registered at their port was falling behind competitors and realized that the economic health of their city depended on internal improvements providing access to the interior wherein lay the future wealth of America. By 1832 Pennsylvania chartered 220 turnpike companies which built some 3,000 miles of roads. Her great state-built canal, 362 miles long and eight years in building, was completed in 1825. Canals were now the cry, and New York was in the lead. To keep up with New York, Philadelphians did all they could to encourage manufacturing, but waterpower for mills was limited, as neither the Delaware nor the Schuylkill had sufficient fall to generate a great amount of power. Steam supplied the alternative, and by 1838 there were more steam engines in Pennsylvania than any other state. The stationary steam engine helped make possible the long step in changing Philadelphia from a commercial to a manufacturing town with all the implications that would make for the city's future. Philadelphia was to have as much steam power as any other American city, steam applied not to ocean-going vessels, but to railroads and factories. With coal and iron in nearby abundance it was inevitable that Philadelphia in her transition from a mercantile center should become a manufacturing center. She had not only the raw materials but she also had the men. John Bristed, in his *Resources of the United States,* published in 1818, noted the city's trend in that direction: "There is no part of the world where, in proportion to its population, a greater number of ingenious mechanics may be found than in the City of Philadelphia or where, in proportion to the capital employed, manufactures thrives better." So great and swift was the rise of factories in Philadelphia that Peter S. Du Ponceau, in toasting the city in 1829, predicted, "Our good city of Philadelphia—In twenty years the Manchester and Lyons of America."

New York City was a busy commercial port after 1800 for the world shipping trade and a logical stopover for coastal sailing vessels. At the lower tip of Manhattan was Battery Park, which Frances Trollope, mother of the English novelist, considered one of the most beautiful city landscapes she visited in her many travels. The spot, with its splendid view, was a favorite promenade for gentlemen and ladies. At little distance to the north, however, was the Five Points, a squalid mess of paupers and prostitutes. Much of the population was transient and cosmopolitan: British and Yankee sailors mingled with Irish and German laborers, Scotch traders, free blacks and slaves; farmers who came into the city before dawn to market produce often spoke Dutch. The normally caustic Mrs. Trollope "enjoyed the elegant hospitality of New York," and concluded that "were all America like this fair city . . . I should say, that the land was the fairest in the world."

I think New York one of the finest cities I ever saw, and as much superior to every other in the Union, (Philadelphia not excepted) as London to Liverpool, or Paris to Rouen. . . . Situated on an island, which I think it will one day cover, it rises, like Venice, from the sea, and like the fairest cities in the days of her glory, receives into its lap tribute of all the riches of the earth. . . . The great defect in the houses is their extreme uniformity—when you have seen one, you have seen all. . . . The luxury of the New York aristocracy is not confined to the city; hardly an acre of Manhatten Island but shews some pretty villa or stately mansion.

Those who settled in the city permanently were businessmen who worked long hours, bent on acquiring wealth and multiplying it. The flavor of the city was highly cosmopolitan and enjoyed, it was reported early in the history of the new nation, "the most eligible situation for commerce in the United States." The *Empress of China* set sail from New York for Canton in 1784, the first American ship to open direct trade with the Orient. George Washington was inaugurated as the nation's first president in New York City on April 30, 1789, at the old City Hall (modernized to accommodate the national government and renamed Federal Hall). The inaugural ceremony attracted a surging mob of people from all around. "The windows and roofs of the houses were crowded," reported one observer, "and in the streets the throng was so dense that it seemed as if one might literally walk on the heads of the people." In its brief but dazzling year before the nation's capital moved to Philadelphia, when it was gloomily predicted that New York would be deserted and revert to a wilderness, social activities reached noteworthy heights. "Public dinners, public days, and private parties may take up a person's whole attention if they attend to them all," John Adams's daughter Abigail complained. As the nineteenth century advanced, New York became the nation's chief seaport, "a great open window to the world," and international commerce that brought imported goods also brought rich crosscurrents of fashion. The bloom of prosperity in this city's ample harbor teeming with craft of every description from all parts of the world was pervasive—New York City was the metropolis on the Hudson.

Shop and Warehouse of Duncan Phyfe, watercolor by J. R. Smith.
THE METROPOLITAN MUSEUM OF ART. ROGERS FUND

During the Federal period, the craft of cabinetmaking was becoming a business. Unquestionably Duncan Phyfe was one of the city's most talented craftsmen, but his workmen made the pieces attributed to his shop or associated with his name. The craft divisions during the Federal period in New York were the cabinet- and chairmakers, making the chairs and case pieces; the inlay makers, specialists with substantial stocks of inlays for sale, some of which they made and some of which they imported; carvers and gilders, making picture frames and looking glasses and carving and gilding furniture; and turners and upholsterers. Such specialization was greatest in cities like New York, but in smaller towns many craftsmen practiced many related trades to make ends meet, doing their own turning, carving, and on occasion upholstering and gilding.

In the 1790s and early 1800s New Yorkers seem to favor several types of chair back designs: shield-back chairs with banisters divided into three splats, centering a fan or Prince-of-Wales feathers with drapery; those with square backs with center banister of angular urn, feathers, and drapery set between vertical colonnettes; and those with three urn splats; and those with four turned colonnettes fanned out at the top to form Gothic

114

arches. After 1805 scroll-back fragile-looking chairs with either turned or outflaring saber legs and cross bars in the back, frequently attributed to the workshop of Duncan Phyfe, came into vogue; less common but surviving in some numbers are chairs with eagle, harp, and lyre backs. Compared to those from other regions, New York chairs have more carving and reeding and less string inlay, and they more generally have a curved medial brace running from the front to the back of the seat frame for support. Instead of slip seats, New York chairs are generally upholstered over the seat rail.

Towards an American Art and Literature

In the long view of history, the Jeffersonian Republic was in abnormally rapid transition. At a speed and in a manner that startled the old nations of Europe from which they and their ancestors had come, Americans moved from apparent insignificance to acknowledged prominence, from shaking beginnings to solid achievements. This "empire of liberty"—of which John Adams, Thomas Jefferson, and their colleagues dreamed and spoke—was dedicated to the beauties of personal liberty, the security of constitutionalism, the rightness of democracy, the wrongness of class distinctions, the virtue of private property, the moral necessity of hard work, the inevitability of progress, and above all the high destiny and glorious future of the United States. In *Redburn*, Herman Melville gave this cosmopolitan belief its noblest expression: "We are not a nation, so much as a world. . . . We are the heirs of all time, and with all nations we divide our inheritance." "We are the Romans of the modern world,—the great assimilating people," mused Oliver Wendell Holmes in *The Autocrat of the Breakfast Table.* Out of such assumptions Americans fashioned an image of themselves as an inclusive nationality, at once diverse and homogeneous, ever improving as it absorbed many types and nationalities of men and women as the new republic forged a unified, superior national culture.

These high expectations were encouraged by the widespread notion that from ancient times, learning, art, and science had progressed geographically from East to West. "Westward the course of empire takes its way," predicted Bishop Berkeley's famous eighteenth-century poem and prophesied "another golden age" of the arts in the New World. Above all, Americans made an automatic connection between political freedom and

Sofa made by Duncan Phyfe for James Lefferts Brinckerhoff in 1816. Like the Grecian cross-front legs on chairs and sofas, the lyre, used as a back splat on chairs and as pedestal base on sewing tables and pier tables, is associated with Phyfe in the decade from 1810 to 1820. The lyre was a decorative motif used so often by Phyfe and his competitors that it is listed and illustrated as a stock item in the 1817 *New-York Book of Prices for Manufacturing Cabinet and Chair Work* as a "Lyre banister" costing seven shillings and eight pence to make. Thirteen of what was originally a set of twenty-four lyre-back chairs, made by Phyfe for the family of William Livingston, governor of New Jersey, are in the Metropolitan Museum of Art, New York. The stylistic features of this sofa appear repeatedly in furniture made by Phyfe: scrolled arms, reeded rails and stiles, caned seats and backs, and gilded volutes and wings.

In 1816 Sarah Huger of New York wrote to relatives in Charleston of her difficulties in getting furniture executed for them by the busy Phyfe, explaining that "Mr. Phyfe is so much the United States rage." Phyfe's workmanship and his interpretation of English Regency forms had become the envy and thus the model for many of his competitors. This sofa is documented in a bill of sale from Phyfe to Brinckerhoff, a New York imported dry goods and crockery merchant, dated October 26, 1816. The cabinetmaking trade was large and competitive in Federal New York City, resulting in a great consistency of styles that makes attributions to a specific maker difficult, if not impossible, unless a piece bears a label or survives with a bill of sale.

intellectual creativity. Surely in a nation without the depressing effect of an authoritarian church or an oppressive political establishment, learning, science, and the arts would flourish as never before. The effect of the War of Independence in Europe was even to make Europeans believe, or feel in a highly emotional way, that they lived in a rare era of momentous change. The success of the Revolution coinciding with the climax of the Enlightenment proved to them that the rights of man and the social contract, of liberty and equality, of responsible citizenship and popular sovereignty, of freedom of thought and speech, separation of powers, and written constitutions could now be made actual among real people. In Europe there was a belief that certain key doctrines were achieving their first realization in the United States. The Venetian ambassador to Paris observed in 1783, "If only the union of the [American Provinces] is preserved, it is reasonable to expect that, with the favorable effects of time, and of European arts and sciences, it will become the most formidable power in the world." Greatness lay in the future, not in the past. "A new Olympus, a new Arcady, a new Athens, a new Greece will perhaps give birth on the continent . . . to new Homers," Abbé Raynal, a French historian and philosopher, predicted.

However, these expectations for America's cultural apotheosis and the impulse to create a national art and literature led to a perplexing dilemma. The United States was still a provincial culture at the beginning of the nineteenth century, dependent on British literature, science, tastes, and standards. How to be great, and at the same time American, was the anxiety-provoking situation for our creative talents. "In relation to the British capital as the centre of English literature, arts, and science," admitted the novelist and editor Charles Brockden Brown in 1801, "the situation of *New and Old-York* may be regarded as the same." The problem for any provincial society is that it looks outside itself for guidance and for standards; it will necessarily be imitative, though also prickly about its tributary status. Cultural pioneers in the new republic had to strike a difficult balance between the traditions of the Old World and the need to break away from them.

In the running discourse in newspapers and periodicals, commencement addresses and political orations, bumptious cultural nationalists called for American ways of writing and painting and of educating the young that would match the political nationalism of James Madison, the economic nationalism of Alexander

Hamilton, and the legal nationalism of John Marshall. "America must be as independent in *literature* as she is in *politics*—as famous for *arts* as for *arms*," the ardent Federalist Noah Webster announced in his famous blue-backed speller. The *North American Review* was founded in Boston by William Tudor, the eldest son of a wealthy Massachusetts mercantile family, "to foster American genius, and, by independent criticism, instruct and guide the public taste," and it soon became the most important intellectual magazine in the country. Modeled on the English critical reviews and specializing in the review essay, it gave considerable space to discussing foreign literature while it aimed to review every important American work, with the reviewers zealously monitoring the American works for faulty grammar or "Americanisms," such as *to advocate, to locate, to fix,* and *progressive.* But in the *North American Review* the American critics were modifying their literary standards and moving away from slavishly following the canons of neoclassical taste. Edward Tyrrell Channing, the younger brother of William Ellery Channing, the Unitarian leader, pleaded in the *North American Review* in 1816 against the timid crampedness produced by writing bound to Augustan models of correct taste. He fused stylistic shift with cultural nationalism: every nation "must be the former and the finisher of its own genius." With ratification of the Treaty of Ghent in 1815 following the War of 1812, the "second war for American independence," Americans looked to the future with fresh confidence and new optimism. Albert Gallatin, Secretary of State and a negotiator of the treaty, observed: "The people . . . are more Americans; they feel and act more as a nation." Some foreign visitors found this assertive pride and fervid nationalism crude and bumptious. The Duc de Lioncourt, touring America in the 1790s, thought there were too many Americans who were "sure nothing good is done, and that no one has any brains, except in America," while a British traveler in 1810 believed that "the national vanity of the United States surpasses that of any other country, not excepting France." "It is impossible to conceive a more troublesome or more garrulous patriotism," wrote Alexis de Tocqueville. "It wearies even those who are disposed to respect it. . . . Nothing is more embarrassing in the ordinary intercourse of life than this irritable patriotism of the Americans." "Our great title is Americans," wrote Tom Paine. And twenty years later Noah Webster reminded his countrymen that "we ought not to consider ourselves inhabitants of a particular state only, but as *Americans.* . . . Every engine should be employed to render the people of this country *national. .* ., and to inspire them with the pride of national character." The literature, like the arts, of the eighteenth century began to appear labored and unnatural, its stately periods a prison and its "Georgian Rule of Taste" "fettered . . . too much by orders, and proportions," a copybook constraint preventing the expression of feeling and spontaneity. The question of what constituted Americanism in a work of literature or art continued to be vexing.

Year after year, as Americans vaunted their country's superiority over decadent Europe and made extravagant claims that their writers were capable of composing an epic equal to the *Aeneid,* scribbling foreign travelers and some trenchant Federalist critics observed that money-grubbing materialism, factious egalitarianism, "vile cupidity," and stern utilitarianism rendered Americans incapable of appreciating or promoting the "agreeable" arts. "To imagine that a refined and classical style of writing will be encouraged here," wrote the high-toned Federalist editor of the *Port Folio,* America's most important literary magazine, "is as absurd as for a thief to break into a Log House in expectation of stealing Silver Tankards." The democratic values of American popular culture unleashed by the Revolution were perceived by the hostile Federalist literati and sniping British critics as a bundle of irreconcilable contradictions. American culture, they said, was a mirage. The most wounding of all criticisms was Sidney Smith's taunt in the *Edinburgh Review* in 1820: "In the four quarters of the globe, who reads an American book? or goes to an American play? or looks at an American picture or statue?"

It was commonly agreed that some institutional solution, some form of patronage was needed to nourish the arts. High culture clearly could not be entirely self-sustaining in the popular marketplace, yet the resources for patronage in the United States seemed unpromising. There were only just beginning to be some very rich men in America during the early years of the Republic, and a few wealthy men did respond to the appeal of cultural leaders of the nation to perform for their society through "liberal patronage" what the Renaissance princes had done for theirs. Aaron Burr, who befriended the twenty-year old John Vanderlyn, financed five years of Paris study for the young artist from 1796 to 1801, and was rewarded by Vanderlyn's success. Philadelphia and New York merchants made Benjamin West's odyssey possible, and Robert Gilmor, a Baltimore patron, assisted Thomas Cole's return to the Old World. Boston merchants set up a trust fund for the artist Washington Allston, who went abroad to study with Benjamin West in London and stayed four years in Paris and Rome before returning to Boston in 1818. At least forty-five American painters and sculptors studied abroad between 1790 and 1830, with probably many more unaccounted for. But the disturbing point that emerged from the soul searching over patronage was the fact that the development of high culture seemed to be retarded by some of the very elements integral to republicanism, namely the absence of a hereditary aristocracy. William Tudor pointed out that in great European families "a splendid gallery of paintings, a magnificent library, descend to the inheritor, with the virtual obligation to cheer genius, to support science, to protect art." This kind of aristocracy was not compatible with American republicanism. In the first decades of nationhood, articulate Americans—perceptive and judgmental, respectful of tradition yet responsive to change, with one foot in the past and the other in the future—backed into the future filled with anxiety and tension. "In this republican society, amid the fluctuating waves of our social life," Nathaniel Hawthorne observed in the *House of Seven Gables*, "somebody is always at the drowning point." It is not surprising that these anxious citizens in pursuit of the "main chance" glanced frantically around for new guidelines of authority and cohesion and endlessly discussed and agonized over republican culture. "How to give all access to the masterpieces of art and nature," Emerson wrote in *The Conduct of Life*, "is the problem of civilization."

Yet the conditions for cultural achievement were by no means absent in the new republic. Cultural life generally depends on cities—where universities, libraries, bookstores, printing presses, newspapers, theaters, and learned societies sustain intellectual interaction—and the new republic certainly had some cities with sufficient population density and wealth to support a lively cultural life. In 1800 Philadelphia, with a population of 70,000, was not only the largest city in America; it was one of the largest cities in the English-speaking world (Edinburgh was not much larger) and seemed set to become the major cultural center of the new republic—though the removal of the political capital to Washington meant that the United States would never have a comprehensive capital city like London or Paris. It possessed a rich and cultivated society, and it was the mecca for French émigrés fleeing first the French Revolution and then Napoleon, many of whom brought with them a taste for the fine and decorative arts. The Franklin Institute of the State of Pennsylvania for the Promotion of the Mechanic Arts was chartered in 1824 and in 1827 staged a public exhibition at which the judges awarded a silver medal to Anthony G. Quervelle, a Paris-born Philadelphian, for a desk and bookcase—"A splendid piece of furniture" made by an "excellent workman." In the early years of the new republic, artists and laymen in Philadelphia and other cities combined to form their own institutions— academies, galleries, art unions, athenaeums, mercantile libraries, and historical societies—to exhibit art and train young artists. In fact, Americans never seemed to tire during these years of "getting up the machinery of Societies," to use Edward Everett's phrase. In 1805, seventy-one of Philadelphia's most distinguished citizens assembled in Independence Hall to draw up a constitution for the Pennsylvania Academy of the Fine Arts. The founders fervently hoped that subscriptions by members, admission receipts, student fees, and commissions from the sale of paintings would enable them to erect a building and purchase antique casts and copies of good paintings. The initial response in "the Athens of America" was overwhelming, but despite their aspirations and bold language, the members soon found themselves locked in artistic jealousies and quarrels. Some artist members opposed the mannerism and artificiality imposed by the exhibition of casts of famous classical works, while others chafed under the lay control imposed on artists by rich patrons and clients. Notwithstanding competition from splinter groups, the carping criticism of American painters who complained they were treated as menials, and even the destruction of its building by fire in 1845, the Pennsylvania Academy remained an influential force in the artistic life of the city. Charles Willson Peale had opened his museum of scientific curiosities in 1786, arranging specimens of living creatures according to the Linnaean classification and employing his artistic skills to paint backgrounds that evoked their habitats.

Bank of Pennsylvania, by Benjamin Henry Latrobe, 1798.
MARYLAND HISTORICAL SOCIETY

At the start of the century, Philadelphia was home to many famous writers, artists, attorneys, and physicians. It was known for its university, its free library, its art academy, and its botanical garden. Its artist colony was the most prominent in the nation: Benjamin Henry Latrobe designed the first Greek Revival building in America, the Bank of Pennsylvania of 1798, and William Rush, the first American sculptor of distinction, was born and worked there. The citizens were proud of their city, and most foreign travelers shared the opinion of the French botanist André Michaux that it was "the most extensive, the handsomest and most populous city in the United States." New York would not be outdone by its southern rival, and after the War of 1812, Philadelphia fell behind New York as a center of national culture. Gentry leaders created the American Academy of Fine Arts in 1802, and in 1804 John Pintard, chief sachem of the Tammany Society, organized the New-York Historical Society. By the late 1820s the American Academy had rolled up large debts, degenerating into a rarely visited depository of old paintings and dust covered statuary; it went bankrupt and was obliged to close its doors. As a result, the National Academy of Design was organized by rebellious New York artists in 1826. Harking back to the glorious days of Renaissance Italy, a speaker at New York's National Academy in 1826 insisted that there was no reason why "the artists of Philadelphia, and Charleston, and Boston, and New York should not feel an honourable rivalship," for it might lead to the same glorious results which the competition among Florence, Rome, and Venice had yielded. The days were gone when foreign painters and returning Americans headed straight for Philadelphia; New York had become the nation's art capital, particularly because of the generosity and patronage of the city's mercantile classes who fought fiercely over building their art collections.

The first serious economic threat to the preeminence of Philadelphia and New York came from the meteoric rise of Baltimore in the Federal period. From the newly opened farmlands of the Susquehanna Valley grain and other produce were floated downriver from as far upstream as the southern counties of New York State. To meet this competition to tap wider hinterlands Philadelphia built the first paved turnpike in America, west to Lancaster in the 1790s; subsquent extensions carried an improved wagon road all the way to the head of the Ohio at Pittsburgh. As seaport cities, both Philadelphia (with tributary streams flowing into the Delaware River) and Baltimore (with the upper reaches of the Patapsco) were on the fall line of waterpower sites that could supply water power for mills. Such a basic source of abundant waterpower, easily accessible, gave each city an incalculable advantage at the beginning of the industrial revolution. Milling wheat Baltimore prospered as the "bread basket" of the young republic. The produce of the western part of Pennsylvania and southern New York went down the Susquehanna River to Port Deposit, at the head of tidewater navigation. There thousands of barrels of wheat, flour, and whiskey, fleets of lumber rafts, and vast quantities of pork and bacon were loaded on schooners for shipment to Baltimore.

In 1820 Baltimore exported 577,000 barrels of flour, exceeding Philadelphia (400,000) and New York (267,000); by 1828, following the completion of the Erie Canal, New York, with 722,000 barrels shipped out, surpassed Baltimore (546,000) and Philadelphia (333,000). During the years that the Chesapeake and Ohio Canal—between Cumberland, Maryland, and Georgetown—was discussed and actually dug, prominent Baltimoreans long had a visionary but impracticable idea of the Susquehanna Canal along the river for upstream navigation. The soundest of Baltimore's canal ideas was for the one connecting Chesapeake and Delaware bays, which today, after successive widenings and deepenings, is a broad sea-level waterway of great value to every port from New York to Norfolk. The rapid development of the West in the nineteenth century was made possible, not by canals and turnpikes, but by two inventions of the Industrial Revolution: the steamboat and the railroad.

Benjamin Henry Latrobe, born in England and trained under the engineer Smeaton and the architect Cockerell, arrived in America in 1796 and in early 1804 received the commission from Bishop John Carroll to design the Roman Catholic Cathedral of Baltimore. Here was a ringing challenge and a magnificent opportunity to prove himself capable of achieving true monumentality in a large building in the Roman design. The Baltimore Cathedral is absolutely unique among Anglo-American buildings on the eastern seaboard in the Federal era. The straightforward use of the traditional Latin cruciform arrangement, with nave and side aisles, the dome rising above the crossing, transcepts and choir is a staunchly Catholic form, but in its construction of a complex system of interrelated vaults and pure geometric spatial organization at the crossing of a cylinder topped by a segmental dome, contained within a cube, the building is the very epitome of English

124

neoclassicism. The Baltimore Cathedral was finally dedicated in 1821, its noble interior and its equally compelling exterior a mute witness to its architect's skill as a consummate engineer in the science of vaulting and also as a sensitive artist with the insights to express and gratify man's highest aspirations.

With ever-increasing ambitions to rival Philadelphia as a cultural center, Baltimoreans saw no reason why their city could not, like Philadelphia, have an impressive structure to house the holdings of the Baltimore Library Company. Latrobe was chosen as the architect and received the commission in 1817, but the money for the library did not materialize because of the financial Panic of 1819. His drawing of the simple neoclassical building of excellent proportions—the chief library room, domed and lighted largely through a glazed cupola, with a gallery around—may well be compared with the Peale Museum, which is still standing. The Peale Museum, a "Museum and Gallery of the Fine Arts" in which Charles Willson Peale's son Raphael placed one of the skeletons of the two mastodons his father had excavated in New York State, was designed by Robert Cary Long in 1813. Baltimore's epithet, "City of Monuments," signifies the pride of its inhabitants in the city's patriotic markers. In 1815 a monument designed by the French-born architect Maximillian Godefroy was dedicated to memorialize the city's defenders who fell in 1814 in the British invasion. In the same year another monument dedicated to the memory of George Washington was designed by Robert Mills in Mount Vernon Square. The single Doric column, 160 feet in height with a statue of Washington atop it, was completed in 1829. Monument-building, as a reminder of the nation's glorious past, became a subject of great interest in a long series of debates and quarreling over the relative merits of obelisks, columns, pyramids, and arches as to their associations and appropriateness as symbols of power, peace, unity, and patriotism. The American Revolution was an event to be defended and glorified, and the men who participated in it must needs be seen as heroes; the Constitution was a Bible which carried the answer to every political exigency, and the men who made it were sacred.

With the election of Thomas Jefferson, America had become a modern nation. The new President stood as a symbol of the new order, and he announced the arrival of a new American era, what he would call "the revolution of 1800." In his First Inaugural Address, he put forth the basic principles of modern liberalism and his visionary belief in America as "the world's best hope," including a commitment to commerce, to continental expansion, and above all to compromise—a pragmatic nonpartisanship in which "we are all republicans: we are all federalists." Jefferson believed in the essential harmony of republican society and in the collective wisdom and moral perceptiveness of the individuals who constituted it. "State a moral case to a ploughman and a professor," he wrote. "The former will decide it as well, and often better, than the latter, because he has not been led astray by artificial rules." Clearly the ploughman—nature's nobleman— surrounded by the majesty and goodness of nature, in Jefferson's view, held an advantage over the isolated professor or the frivolous aristocrat. America in 1800 was paradoxically both a classical republic and a modern nation, and Jefferson himself epitomized that turbulent transition: he was the eighteenth-century philosopher who became the nineteenth-century pragmatist, the agrarian turned capitalist, localist turned nationalist, small-republic republican turned continental expansionist. For America as well, the transition was troubling, an uneasy accommodation between the old and the new, between the nostalgic traditionalists seeking to revive a long lost republican society and eager innovators in search of a liberal utopia, particularly for those who marched ahead into the future fearfully in search of a political and cultural theory, always looking backward with an eye to the past. While American leaders sought desperately to keep the dream alive with technological promises and nostalgic memories, the doubts remained.

Once begun, the War of 1812 had a profound effect on American life. The successful Treaty of Ghent and Andrew Jackson's great victory at New Orleans stimulated economic development, government centralization, and nationalist fervor. Henry Adams remarked nearly a hundred years ago that the peace announcement turned attention from issues that had dominated the public agenda for a generation: "A people which had in 1787 been indifferent or hostile to roads, banks, funded debt, and nationality had become in 1815 habituated to ideas and machinery of that sort on a great scale," he wrote. The belief that the citizens of the American Israel were God's chosen people had intensified and hardened in the crucible of war. War did not simply cause nor result from liberalizing change in America, but instead reflected it, intensified it, and ultimately legitimized it. And as Edmund Burke once wrote, "War never leaves where it found a nation."

Opposite Late eighteenth-century embroidered needlework and sewing implements in the Chester County Historical Society, West Chester, Pennsylvania.

The Livingston-Backus House, Genesee Country Village, Mumford, New York, built in Rochester, New York, by James Livingston, in 1827; the Methodist Church, built in the hamlet of Brooks Grove, New York, in 1844. The completion of the Erie Canal in 1825 had a momentous effect upon Genesee Country; along the canal established cities prospered and new towns sprang up. As the wheat from Genesee farmers poured into Rochester's great merchant mills, barge loads of barreled flour headed for the eastern markets. One of the entrepreneurs who fashioned a fortune from milling, banking, and speculative ventures was James Livingston, a descendant of the Hudson River family. His Greek Revival mansion, built in 1827, was sold to Joseph Strong in 1835, who in turn sold it to Dr. Frederick Backus in 1838. The Greek Revival Brooks Grove Church, with its three-stage bell tower, was built on land originally purchased from Mary Jemison, "the White Woman of Genesee," who lived her entire life with the Indians.

Greek Revival dwelling from Waterville, New York, at the Genesee Country Village, Mumford, New York, built about 1847, the birthplace of George Eastman, founder of Eastman Kodak Company; the Ezra Jones farmhouse, built in the town of Orleans, New York, about 1820. The Greek Revival style was symbolic: for liberal-thinking Jacksonians the use of Greek patterns was a reminder of the democratic ideals of the people of ancient Greece and a tangible indication of American sympathy for the Greek struggle for independence from the Turks (1821–32). The architectural handbooks of Asher Benjamin and Minard Lafever enabled country carpenters, working with a "saw in one hand and a book of instructions in the other," to provide their clients with houses and churches in the latest fashion with Greek massing and bold detail. By the 1830s a Greek Revival vernacular, particularly in domestic architecture, had developed fully in central and western New York State. As a visiting British architect reported from New York in 1835, "The Greek mania here is at its height, as you infer from the fact that everything is a Greek temple, from the privies in the back court, through the various grades of prison, church, custom house, and state-house."

Romulus Female Seminary, Genesee Country Village, Mumford, New York, built about 1855 in Romulus, New York. Beginning early in the nineteenth century, private (sometimes referred to as "Select") schools for young ladies were established in many western New York villages and towns, where the course of study included literature, foreign languages, and science, as well as music, needlework, art, and penmanship. This was in part to give the girls educational opportunities equal to those offered at the boys' private academies and in part because of the concern of church groups to provide what they considered appropriate instruction for young ladies. Built toward the end of the Greek Revival period, this one-story building includes the basic elements of that style: two square columns are topped by a wide entablature which, in turn, is capped by a pediment with full returns of the cornice. The seminary closed in 1883, and the building was bought by the Presbyterian Church.

View from the dining room into the parlor of the John MacKay Homestead, built in 1814 in Caledonia, New York, Genesee Country Village, Mumford, New York. In the late eighteenth century, a number of Scots settled near the "Big Springs" at the site of present-day Caledonia, along the war path of the Iroquois between the Finger Lakes and the Niagara frontier. MacKay, a canny Scot from Pennsylvania, acquired mill sites, built a malt house, and prospered sufficiently to build a two-story brick-lined Federal house. The elegant three-bay façade is articulated by four pilasters linked by blind elliptical arches. Much of the millwork and some of the furniture for MacKay's house was fashioned by Horace and Chester Harding, cabinetmakers and chairmakers in Caledonia (the latter became a portrait painter). The scrolled-arm fancy Sheraton settee, seen through the door, is attributed to an Albany maker, about 1810. John MacKay's portrait hangs over the original mantel in the dining room; the fireboard is a reproduction.

Musical instruments at Sunnyside, Tarrytown, New York, built in the late seventeenth century and remodeled by Washington Irving, 1835–37. Irving's nieces, Catherine Ann and Sarah Irving, played on this piano, which was made by Robert Nunns, Clark and Company in New York City between 1833 and 1838. Their book of music rests on one of its music stands. Irving celebrated Christmas at Sunnyside, often surrounded by members of his family. His letters are filled with references to the holiday and descriptions of Sunnyside decked with greens in the manner of an English country house such as the one described in his novel *Bracebridge Hall* of 1822.

South façade of Wyck, Germantown, Pennsylvania, built between 1690 and 1824. The oldest house in Germantown, Wyck stands on property owned by nine generations of the same Quaker family. In 1824 William Strickland, architect of the Second Bank of the United States, blended the interiors of two earlier houses into a single mansion without altering the colonial appearance of the exterior. By removing interior walls and windows, Strickland created four large rooms on the first floor and introduced spatial and functional flexibility to the house, demonstrating his talent for adapting an old building using historically sympathetic yet conveniently modern designs for space and light. He installed glazed sliding doors in the north and south walls of the hall, forming a conservatory that was sunlit both summer and winter. The setting of the renovated house was enhanced by the addition of an ornamental rose garden on the north lawn.

Opposite

Library at Upsala, Germantown, Pennsylvania, built in 1798 for John Johnson. Just opposite Benjamin Chew's Cliveden, this grand Federal mansion is the fitting culmination of the Anglicization of one of Germantown's most prominent eighteenth-century families. Johnson, the great-grandson of Dirk Jansen, an early German settler and an owner of Wyck at the beginning of the eighteenth century, married Sarah Wheeler, a woman of English ancestry. Paint analysis has revealed that the library was originally painted this lively combination of peach, mustard, maroon, and white. The mantel was exquisitely chip-carved with swags, rosettes, and shields. The fireplace surround is locally quarried King of Prussia marble. The walnut candlestand was made in Philadelphia about 1790, but the Colonial revival side chair dates to about 1880; both descended in the Johnson family. The English engraving *Conquered But Not Subdued* by Thomas Faed is dated 1866.

139

Bedroom at Upsala. The mahogany bed in this room is
Colonial revival, while the doll's bed was a birthday present
to Johnson's daughter Elizabeth in 1811, one of his nine
children. The mahogany washstand was made in
Philadelphia about 1790 and the fancy chair about 1810.
The brass andirons are early nineteenth-century American.

Screen of Doric columns in the entrance hall at Cliveden, Germantown, Pennsylvania, built for Benjamin Chew, 1763–67. At Cliveden, Chew built a country house appropriate to his position as chief justice of the supreme court of Pennsylvania and trusted advisor to the Penns and commodious enough for his large family. The building is an outstanding example of mid-Georgian architecture in the neo-Palladian style adapted to colonial tastes and fashion. The portrait of Margaret Oswald was painted by John Wollaston in 1758; Margaret's sister Elizabeth married Benjamin Chew and this portrait is said to have always hung in this place of honor. Beneath it is a lyre-base mahogany card table, one of a pair, made in Philadelphia about 1810. Cliveden did not fare well during the Revolution. In October 1777 it was transformed into a fortress when British soldiers under General William Howe took refuge there after firing on Washington's advancing troops in the Battle of Germantown. The patriots were unable to breach Cliveden's solid walls, but after their retreat Chew found his country house "an absolute wreck."

Nineteenth-century Quaker bonnets in the Chester County Historical Society, West Chester, Pennsylvania. The goal of Quaker religious life was to find God in the simplicity of the Inner Light, characterized by quietism and the plain life; the Quaker stripped his worship to the stark simplicity of silent communion in a bare meetinghouse. There, in a plain structure furnished with rows of plain benches, waited in silence a plainly dressed people—men in broad-brimmed hats and lapel-less shad-bellied coats and women in coal-scuttle bonnets, plain shawls, and dove-gray gowns, stripped of all superfluities and useless ornaments—until someone was moved to speak the words that the divine spirit vouchsafed to him or her for the edification of the group. Perhaps in some measure we owe to the plainness of the Quaker way of life something of the soundness of workmanship, the sureness of line, and the studied avoidance of over-elaborate decoration found in the best craftsmanship of the Federal period.

Upsala was built on land that had been in the Jansen/Johnson family for four generations. The house is almost square with the principal façade ornamented by a marble belt course and marble lintels above the windows. The interior is laid out in the classic center hall plan with four rooms on each floor; their chip-carved mantelpieces and paneled wainscoting are particularly notable. Upsala represents the change from the traditional German architecture found in early eighteenth-century Germantown and the hybrid Anglo-German style of mid-century to the Federal style country seat of a wealthy English gentleman at the end of the century.

Conyngham-Hacker House, Germantown, Pennsylvania, built in 1796 by William Forbes, a native of Aberdeenshire, Scotland. Germantown, founded in 1683 by thirteen Quaker families from Germany with a common desire to participate in William Penn's "holy experiment," retains the diversity of population and the extraordinary domestic architecture that have been a prominent part of its history since the eighteenth century. By 1735 there were congregations of Mennonites, Brethren (also known as Dunkers and German Baptists), Lutherans, and German Reformed, in addition to the Quakers. Papermaking and printing helped Germantown remain a distinctively German community through most of the eighteenth century. In the 1790s repeated yellow-fever epidemics in Philadelphia drove all those who could afford it to build or rent summer houses in Germantown. Forbes, a well-to-do Philadelphia merchant, built this summer house in 1796; on his death in 1801 it was rented for many years to David Hayfield Conyngham. In 1844 the property was bought by Isaiah Hacker, who undertook major alterations and additions a decade later.

Opposite

Slant-front desk, made in Westmoreland County, in southwestern Pennsylvania, about 1800, made and inlaid with local woods: cherry, white pine, poplar, walnut, and maple stringing. Southwestern Pennsylvania, separated from the rest of the state by the Allegheny Mountains, became a furniture-making center during the Federal period. The area was well established with a stable population drawn by good land, coal, forests, and the emergence of iron and glass industries. Philadelphia and Baltimore were the most direct influences on the furniture made there during the Federal period. The predominant woods were cherry and walnut, until the completion of the National Road in 1819 made imported mahogany available. Samuel Brown, a Westmoreland County cabinetmaker, advertised in 1801 that "he is enabled to supply those who will favour him with their custom, in any fashion of Walnut or Cherry Furniture, either ornamented or plain. . . . inlayed of whatever figure may be called for." The inlay pattern most characteristic of southwestern Pennsylvania is the vine-and-leaf, emanating from a vase or urn at the base and terminating in several leaves, pomegranates, or flowers.

Iahogany chest of drawers made by Jonathan Gostelowe, hiladelphia, 1783–93, now at Cliveden, Philadelphia. Gostelowe is best known for his monumental, serpentine-front chests of drawers with canted corners. The 1762 edition of Thomas Chippendale's *Gentleman and Cabinet-Maker's Director* illustrates similar chests with ogee bracket feet. English chests of the 1750s and 1760s display the elaborate carving and robust forms of the prevailing rococo style. By the 1770s canted corners were ornamented only with reeding, fluting, or fretwork, or were left plain. Gostelowe's chest is a consciously restrained version of earlier English designs, typical of the early Federal period.

President's House, Western Reserve College, Hudson, Ohio, designed by Lemuel Porter and completed in 1830. Hudson has often been described, with reason, as a transplanted New England town. In a section of northeastern Ohio that was part of Connecticut until 1800, much of the territory was known as the Western Reserve. Lemuel Porter, a Connecticut-born carpenter-builder, designed this two-family Georgian house for the president and the professor of theology of the college in a style typical of earlier Connecticut houses, embellished with Federal details in the graceful recessed doorways.

Cupboard made in Madison Township, Montgomery County, Ohio, by Christian Shiveley, Jr., between 1810 and 1820. Born in Maryland, Shiveley moved to Pennsylvania with his parents before migrating to western Ohio in 1804. Six of these massive cupboards by Shiveley are known, all distinguished by their bold proportions, elaborate crown moldings, and neatly scrolled brackets. Ohio was settled quickly during the first half of the nineteenth century, and among the new residents were skilled craftsmen, such as Shiveley, seeking more lucrative markets for their wares. In some cases, their work can be readily identified by construction techniques and decorative details as in the magnificent cupboards made by Christian Shiveley.

149

Edgewater, Barrytown, New York, built by John Robert Livingston about 1820 for his daughter Margaret and son-in-law, Captain Lowndes Brown of Charleston, South Carolina, and attributed on stylistic grounds to Robert Mills. The massive classical portico, with six Doric columns supporting a wide entablature decorated with triglyphs and mutules were features favored by Mills. The long arched windows are set in brick walls bisected by a masonry stringcourse. Robert Donaldson purchased the house in 1852, and two years later Alexander Jackson Davis designed the octagonal library at the left.

Opposite

Entrance hall of Edgewater. Margaret Livingston Brown, châtelaine of Edgewater for some thirty years, possessed not only a beautiful house but exalted family connections. Life on the banks of the Hudson, where there were such diversions as boating, picnics, balls, and amateur theatricals, must have been very pleasant. The stylish nineteenth-century geometric design was painted on the hall floor by the Canadian artist Robert Jackson in 1980.

150

Dining room at Edgewater. The Empire dining table was made in New York City about 1825; the six side chairs around it, made by Phyfe, came from the family of Chancellor Robert R. Livingston, an uncle of Mrs. Lowndes Brown. The girandole over the mantel, which resembles the pair in the drawing room, descended in the Ten Eyck family. The centerpiece of about 1820 with bisque figures supporting a porcelain fruit basket is French.

Overleaf

The enfilade of dining room, drawing room, and library of
Edgewater. The pair of sixteen-light crystal chandeliers,
made in England about 1830, hang from elaborate plaster
rosettes in the dining room and drawing room. A Swedish
traveler, Frederika Bremer, who visited the Hudson River
Valley in 1849, described the opulence and tranquility of
life there. Of the entertainment the Donaldsons gave in her
honor she commented, "The assembly was beautiful and gay,
and the breakfast, which was magnificent, was closed by a
dance."

Small red sitting room off the entrance hall of Edgewater.
The portrait of Robert Donaldson's wife, Susan, was painted
by George Cooke in 1832. The window seats (one of which is
depicted in the painting) were made by Duncan Phyfe,
possibly in 1822. The harp (which also appears in the
painting), was made in London in the early nineteenth
century. The bust of Washington over the door is a plaster
copy of the portrait by Jean Antoine Houdon.

154

View of the red sitting room at Edgewater. The elegant Federal mahogany and satinwood fall-front desk of about 1810 is attributed to Phyfe. Above it hangs a portrait of John Peter Van Ness by Gilbert Stuart.

Opposite

Drawing room at Edgewater. Here there are seven side chairs and a mahogany sofa attributed to Duncan Phyfe with curule legs ending in gilded brass paws. The grand pair of girandoles or convex mirrors, surmounted by eagles and cornucopias, was made in Albany about 1815 for the De Peyster family of that city. Beneath them are a pair of neoclassical New York pier tables, with stenciled decorations and marble columns, that came from the Livingston family.

North bedroom of Edgewater. The bed, cheval glass, sofa, and chest of drawers are New York pieces of the 1820s and 1830s, and show the French influence on late American neoclassical design. The massive mahogany desk and bookcase, embellished with gilding and stenciling, is attributed to Joseph Meeks and Sons of New York City. The plaster bust in the window is of Robert Fulton.

158

Library at Edgewater, the octagonal addition designed by Alexander Jackson Davis in 1854. The sofa in the foreground, the Grecian couch on the right, and the worktable at its head were made for Donaldson by Phyfe, probably in 1822. The armchairs flanking the fireplace and the center table are New York Empire pieces.

Andalusia on the Delaware River north of Philadelphia, built as a summer house in 1797–98 for John and Margaret Murphy Craig; enlarged by Benjamin Henry Latrobe as a country seat between 1806 and 1808; and again between 1834 and 1836 after their daughter Jane married Nicholas Biddle. Thomas U. Walter, the Biddle family architect and master of the Greek Revival style, remodeled the house into a colossal Doric porticoed temple. As a scholar, writer, and orator, the precocious Biddle attracted local attention. Graduating from Princeton in 1801 at the age of fifteen with the highest honors, he read law, and then in 1804 went off to Paris as secretary to the American minister. There he attended Napoleon's coronation, traveled extensively in Italy, and was the first American to visit Greece in the pure and simple role of a tourist. Contemplating the remains of ancient temples, he seized with the lasting conviction that there were only two perfect truths in the world—the Bible and Greek architecture. His European wanderings ended in London, where he served as secretary to James Monroe before returning to Philadelphia in 1807.

Plaster ceiling decoration and ormolu chandelier in the yellow parlor at Andalusia. The chandelier, one of a pair ordered for the house, decorated with putti playing musical instruments, was acquired by Edward Craig Biddle for his parents from Thomire et Cie in 1836. The other chandelier is in the library.

Italian marble mantel and Philadelphia overmantel in the
yellow parlor at Andalusia. This room was remodeled by the
Biddles' architect Thomas U. Walter. The mantel and mirror
were ordered especially for the house by Biddle. If any
period of time in the history of a great city may be linked
with the name of a single one of its citizens, Philadelphia in
the years 1825 to 1840, years of impressive growth and
prosperity for the city, is the age of Nicholas Biddle.

Dining room at Andalusia, in the part of the house designed by Latrobe. Walter incorporated several of Latrobe's exterior windows into his addition; one of them is visible in the backround here, with a view through into the Ottoman parlor. The American furniture in the dining room is mahogany and dates from about the 1830s. The nineteenth-century *vieux Paris* porcelain and the silver made by Thomas Charles Fletcher in Philadelphia belonged to the Biddles.

Library of Andalusia, part of Thomas U. Walter's enlargement of the house for Nicholas Biddle. The bookcases, with their original and painted decoration, contain much of Biddle's book collection. The inlaid and gilded mahogany center table was made in Philadelphia or Baltimore, about 1800–1850. The ormolu chandelier was made by Thomire et Cie of Paris in 1836 and is one of two ordered for the house by the Biddles' son. Andalusia is replete with neoclassical details, among the most beautiful being these bookcases in the library. Biddles' descendants became "men of business," as Sidney George Fisher expressed it, worthy gentlemen content to live in quiet ease on inherited wealth, while Biddle himself devoted his life to "always seeing and achieving result."

Painted and stenciled settee made in Zanesville, Ohio, by James Huey between 1830 and 1840. Furniture made in Ohio during the first half of the nineteenth century reflects the state's position as a crossroads of American cultural traditions. The first state formed from the Northwest Territory, Ohio became the new home of people from the original thirteen states as well as Kentucky and Tennessee, and the simple, household furniture made there reflects the diverse heritage of those settlers. This fancy settee is stenciled J. HUEY/ZANESVILLE on the bottom of the seat. Huey advertised his chair factory in the *Ohio Republican* in May 1829, "where he intends keeping on hand a general assortment of Grecian, Windsor, Fancy, and Common chairs made in the latest and most approved fashions." Furniture making was well established in Ohio by 1850: the census listed nearly 500 cabinetmakers in the state. By that time Huey's steam-powered cabinet and chair factory employed twenty men and produced $8,000 worth of furniture annually.

Upstairs hallway of Chipstone, Fox Point, Wisconsin, north of Milwaukee, overlooking Lake Michigan, built in 1950 for Mr. and Mrs. Stanley Stone, and designed by Andrew Hepburn of the Boston firm of Perry, Shaw, and Hepburn in the colonial revival style. Under the circular window is a New Hampshire bow-front mahogany chest of drawers, made about 1790 to 1810. Beyond it is a Massachusetts mahogany block-front bureau table of 1760–80. Between the case pieces are a Philadelphia side chair and an elegant Massachusetts table, both in the Chippendale style.

The Democratic Age of Jackson
in the Old South

171

BY 1820 THE EIGHTEENTH-CENTURY WORLD of the founding fathers expired completely, to be replaced by the nineteenth-century world of democracy, individualism, and capitalist development. James Monroe's presidency (1816–24) brought a deceptive calm to American politics, an age of cooperation and collective purpose, lacking the bitter partisanship of earlier years—an "Era of Good Feelings," as one Boston newspaper had rejoiced. With the world at peace, Americans were less distracted by issues and devoted themselves to economic development and the settlement of the continent. The pace of economic change quickened as states turned to the development of transportation networks and proliferated their grants of corporate power, harnessing private enterprise to public goals. Expansive, self-assertive, extravagantly optimistic, the American people in a nation of infinite promise believed they had a God-given right to pursue happiness. There were no permanent barriers of distinctions of rank to the people's aspirations for wealth and self-improvement. Nothing struck Tocqueville more forcibly when he visited the United States in 1831 than this leveling of ancient and inherited distinctions of rank. While Americans showed no interest in economic leveling, they were increasingly demanding equality of esteem. Tocqueville and other foreign visitors were amazed by the egalitarian tone of American society, its belligerent disregard of conventional social distinctions. Terms like "gentleman" and "lady" might be claimed by anyone. Somehow this drive for individual self-betterment, as Tocqueville repeatedly emphasized, had thus far managed to avoid anarchy while greatly expanding most people's possibilities of life.

The calm did not last. The forces of modernization and social change accelerated, intensifying the strains on American unity, and this market society and short-lived Jeffersonian Republican consensus began to fragment even at the moment of its consolidation. The 1820s opened with two dark portents: the Panic of 1819 and the Missouri crisis. The panic introduced Americans to the cyclical fluctuations of boom-and-bust of a modernizing economy, and every section of the country was hit hard, particularly the South. Banks failed and dragged down with them merchants, businessmen, and farmers who were deeply in debt. The Missouri Compromise was triggered by the request of Missouri late in 1819 for admission as a state in which slavery would be permitted. At the time, there were twenty-two states, evenly divided between slave and free. Admission of Missouri as a slave state would have upset that balance and set a precedent for congressional

172

condoning of the expansion of slavery. An extraordinarily bitter debate erupted in the Senate and the House. When deadlock threatened, a compromise bill was worked out with the provisions that Missouri was admitted as a slave state and Maine (formerly part of Massachusetts) as free, and, except for Missouri, slavery was to be excluded from the Louisiana Purchase lands north of latitude 36°30'—the line between Missouri and the Arkansas Territory. The act helped hold the Union together for more than thirty years, but the controversy shook the South's faith in the integrity and goodwill of the rest of the nation. "The Union is part of the religion of this people," Emerson said, but the debates over Missouri revealed fundamentally divergent attitudes toward its nature and, indeed, about the meaning of freedom and equality. The compromise avoided any decision on the future or morality of slavery itself, but it left as a legacy a new feature defining the geography of the continent: a clear line of latitude dividing slavery and freedom. Reflecting on the Missouri crisis in his diary, John Quincy Adams commented, "The seeds of the Declaration of Independence are yet maturing. The harvest will be what [Benjamin] West, the painter, calls the terrible and sublime."

For many Southerners, the attempt to bar slavery from new states, coinciding with the growing power of the federal judiciary by the charter of the Second Bank of the United States and the plans for centrally funded internal improvements, revived Republican fears about consolidation. To Jefferson, in retirement, the move to restrict slavery in Missouri was a cynical plot by Federalists trying to destroy southern interests. Out of generalized fears of consolidation fused with the particular need to protect slavery, a romantic legend began to envelop the South—the Old South, the solid South, the united South—dominated by slavery and cotton, monolithic in its interests, a nation within a nation.

The South has many images. When Americans think of its past, they may call to mind the stereotype of white-columned plantation mansions, courtly planters leisurely quaffing mint juleps and beautifully dressed southern belles strolling in shady gardens, and contented and deferential slaves harvesting white cotton fields—an era forever "gone with the wind." The Old South of popular legend, wrote Wilbur J. Cash, "was a sort of stage piece out of the eighteenth century, wherein gesturing gentlemen moved soft-spokenly against a background of rose gardens and dueling grounds, through always gallant deeds; and lovely ladies, in farthingales, never for a moment lost that exquisite remoteness which has been the dream of all men and the possession of none."

But there were poor rural whites—proud, ambitious, aggressive—eking out a living on worn-out fields. They might be chivalric and gentle, but they could also be downright unruly and unmoral. There was also a plain-folk democracy of middle-class farmers—the yeomen—who were generally non-slaveholders and reasonably well-educated, a class that owned their fair share of the land and prospered. They were the people who worked hard, played hard, laughed loudly, and aspired to improve themselves both materially and spiritually. They were the backbone of antebellum southern society. This rich and diverse tapestry of the Old South—some famous, most obscure, but all playing a role in the shaping of southern civilization—is vast and paradoxical. The Old South was indeed distinct, as were the North and West and mid-Atlantic states, a beleaguered region of extraordinary variation and complexity, a dream world, a pastoral society seeking to hold to a way of life that was destined not to endure.

Virginia Capitol: End elevation, by Thomas Jefferson.
MASSACHUSETTS HISTORICAL SOCIETY. COOLIDGE COLLECTION

While the Old South was primarily an agricultural region of backcountry-lowcountry contrasts, several large cities and numerous small and medium-sized towns existed. Washington, Richmond, Charleston, Mobile, and New Orleans had significant populations in comparison to other urban centers outside the region, and they were the locus of change in that slowly evolving society. During the pre-Civil War period the South rapidly became urbanized. Not to be overlooked in any assessment of the South's society were city and town dwellers, many of whom were businessmen, traders, shopkeepers, shippers, skilled and common laborers, editors, and professionals, including lawyers, teachers, medical doctors, and ministers. While their numbers were small by comparison to those engaged in agriculture, they were a necessary part of the economy, holding high social and economic positions in the towns and surrounding countryside. In the romantic legend of the Old South, large cities such as Charleston and New Orleans have had a great place, but the ordinary towns and cities have been ignored, almost as if they did not exist. Yet these cities and towns deserve close scrutiny. The significant minority who made their living indirectly from agriculture (cotton factory and warehouse owners, farm implement dealers, and mule traders) could not have existed without the vitality of the agrarian life. In the cities the signs of the breaking down of slavery emerged as the result of the hiring system and the relaxing of agrarian opposition to a protective tariff because of the introduction of factories. The development of urban communities suggests that antebellum southern society was more diverse, dynamic, and democratic than prevailing stereotypes would admit.

Their friends and relatives might have been obliged to be planters, but the young professionals were urban in the antebellum South. The development of urban communities made possible the establishment of schools, lyceums, public libraries, and theaters, providing cultural advantages for the citizens. As early as 1748 the Charleston Library Society, modeled after the Royal Society of London, had been organized by seventeen citizens hoping "to save their descendants from sinking into savagery." A college opened in 1790 and the Charleston Theater, built in 1793, gave an inaugural performance of *The Tragedy of the Earl of Essex* the following year. In the decade of the 1790s Charleston could support a symphony orchestra, two fine theater orchestras, a chorus for the opera, and excellent singers.

The founding of the Charleston Museum in 1773 was an attempt to establish a center for the study of science, particularly through the contributions of the physicians in the city. Most of them had been trained abroad and were directed toward the exotic plants of the South for vegetable remedies by their correspondence with Europeans interested in natural history. In 1839 when James Silk Buckingham, a British traveler, lectured in Charleston on Palestine and Egypt, he noted that his lectures were attended by larger audiences in proportion to the population than in any other city where he had spoken and that they were better reported by the Charleston newspapers. But the lyceum movement and its lectures did not take root in the South as strongly as it did in the North, partly because in the North there existed a close connection between this institution and the various reform movements, especially the abolition movement. Furthermore, Southerners, with their love of rhetoric and their interest in oratory in politics, prefered debating societies to didactic lectures, which were the staple of northern lyceums.

View Along the East Battery, Charleston, by S. Barnard, 1831.
YALE UNIVERSITY ART GALLERY. MABEL BRADY GARVAN COLLECTION

By 1820 the depletion of the soil in coastal areas of Virginia and Maryland and declining population and wealth brought prolonged agricultural depression as tobacco had given way to wheat (and flour milling) and wheat to diminishing yields of corn. And by 1830 the towns of the lower seaboard South were beginning to exhibit signs of decline and decay; the falling demand for traditional staples led Southern planters, with their heavy investment in slaves, to a frantic search for new agricultural exports, and they found it in cotton production. The commercial potential of a single crop so dominated southern life that other types of enterprise were neglected and guaranteed that the South would remain an essentially rural and agricultural society tied together by an extraordinary reliance on cotton produced by the labor of hundreds of thousands of black slaves. The slave and agricultural base of southern planter society, together with the peculiarities of the marketing system for cotton, prevented the rise of the multitudes of small commercial communities that were fragmenting and democratizing the society of the North. Understandably, Southerners led the way in the rush for western land. The technological perfection of the cotton gin and the screw press for compression of cotton into bales, the rapid proliferation of steamboats opening the way to upriver navigation on the Mississippi and the rich network of other southern waterways, and the southern planters' ability to move quickly and easily large units of labor—their slaves—to the most promising markets in the West resulted in the southwestern agricultural expansion in which King Cotton reigned.

By 1840 the South produced more than 60 percent of the world's cotton and by the 1850s American cotton supplied the rising industries of continental Europe; well over half this output went to the textile mills of Great Britain. Between 1836 and 1840 cotton accounted for 63 percent of the value of all America's exports. For a time cotton made New Orleans the nation's leading seaport in value of exports. As the demand increased, the South's dependency on slavery and the fortunes of a single crop deepened. Wherever new lands were cleared, where expenses were low and the soil still good, slaves and their owners poured in. For those who remained in the exhausted lowlands of Georgia and South Carolina, hard times closed in. During a tour in 1831 the poet William Gilmore Simms wrote of Savannah, "Like most of our Southern townships and depots it remains stationary and has an air of utter languishment." He attributed this condition to the relative decline of cotton culture in the seaboard slave states. Charleston impressed the actress Fanny Kemble as a place with an air of genteel decay and eccentricity, a closed city which rendered its citizens indifferent to outside criticism and freed them from "devotion to conformity in small things and great, which pervades the American body-social from the matter of church-going to the trimming of women's petticoats."

With the future bleak, the city in economic decline, and old fears revitalized by an abortive slave rebellion in Charleston in June 1822, the citizens turned to their historic past for reassurance. To those Northerners who charged that slavery was a relic of a barbaric past, Southerners pointed to ancient Greece and Rome. Classical civilizations had achieved greatness because the slaveholder was free to cultivate the intellect, not spend his days in worrisome, menial labor. Without slaves, the Parthenon could not have been built, the pyramids could not have been raised. "We must recollect," proclaimed Thomas Roderick Dew, professor of political economy at William and Mary College, in 1832, "that the *laws* of Lycurgus were promulgated, the sublime eloquence of Demosthenes and Cicero was heard, and the glorious achievements of Epaminondas and Scipio were witnessed, in countries where slavery existed—without *for one moment* loosening the tie between master and slave." The southern defense of slavery took many forms, and the idea that slavery encouraged, not retarded, the march of civilization was given a different basis in 1837 by William Harper of South Carolina. Slave labor was essential to the production of cotton, he argued, and "cotton has contributed more than anything else of later times to the progress of civilization. By enabling the poor to obtain cheap and becoming clothing, it has inspired a taste for comfort, the first stimulus to civilization."

In such a society, where thoughts were freezing into a permanent form, where the living were developing a certain reverence for the past, what was the place of education? Thomas Smith Grimké, who supported the Charleston colonization movement to send the Negroes back to Africa, was a militant anticlassicist and almost alone among his contemporaries in expounding a theory of pragmatic education that would act as a bridge to the future. In a speech in Charleston in 1827 and in another at Yale three years later, he attacked education "on the Catholic principle" that students "must read with a submissive faith, that they must believe *all* in Homer and Virgil, in Horace and Theocritus to be poetry—*all* in Cicero and Demosthenes to be eloquence— *all* in Thucydides and Herodotus, in Livy and Tacitus, to be unrivalled in History." He attacked rote memorization of the classics advocating education based "on the Protestant principle" that one must "think and reason" for oneself. Such vociferous anticlassicism from Grimké, living in this proud city of Greek Revival architecture but in decline and losing population (while its rival New Orleans was growing rapidly), reveals the ambivalence of Americans toward classical learning. An anonymous New Yorker in 1835 declared "there

178

is not a country on earth where there is less reverence for antiquity than in the United States," a judgment confirmed about the same time by Tocqueville: "Democratic Communities . . . care but little for what occurred at Rome and Athens."

No one better defined this ambivalence than Hugh Swinton Legaré, who took up Grimké's challenge in his first article in the *Southern Review,* defending classical learning against modern or scientific learning. According to Legaré, one should study in order to observe beauty, not to improve the condition of mankind. One should study the beauty that is eternal in nature. "Suppose the object described to be twilight," he wrote in a review of Lord Byron's letters. "Any one who doubts what is obvious to reason, may convince himself by comparing parallel passages in the ancient and modern classics—e.g., Milton's lines, 'Now came still evening on, and twilight gray', Virgil's beautiful verses on midnight, in the fourth *Aeneid,* Homer's on moonlight in the eighth *Iliad.* The exquisite sketches are all in precisely the same style, and if they were in the same language, might easily be ascribed to the same age of poetry." This southern romantic admired the unity of purpose, simplicity of style, and ease of execution of classical Roman texts. Aware of the decline of Charleston, Legaré wrote a friend in melancholy in 1833: "*We* are (I am quite sure) the *last* of the *race* of South-Carolina; I see nothing before us but decay and downfall,—but, on that account, I cherish its precious relics the more." When he heard of the death of Grimké in 1834, he paused to reflect in his exile in Brussels, where he was American chargé d'affaires:

The worst of it is that, as such persons have never been produced anywhere else in America than in the low country of South-Carolina, so that soil is now worn out, and, instead of these oaks of the forest, its noble original growth, is sending up, like its old fields left to run to waste, thickets of stunted loblolly pine, half choked with broom grass and dog fennel. Take it all together, there are few spectacles so affecting as the decay of our poor parish country, which I often think of, even at this distance, with the fondness of disappointed love.

Such elegy as prophecy, antediluvian in the midst of the freshet of the nullification controversy (pitting Jackson against Calhoun over whether a state could nullify federal law) and before the flood of civil war, reflected Charleston's mood of alienation and romanticism at the moment when the city sensed the pain of separation from the Revolutionary generation. Calhoun died in 1850 and the city honored him, but his legacy, the ultimate defense of secession, was not enough. The war came, and the city lay in ruins.

When the South Carolinian Charles Pinckney declared in 1787, "When I say Southern, I mean Maryland, and the states to the southward of her," he was expressing a point of view not uncommon in the post-Revolutionary South. The terms South, Middle, North, and West were spoken and written without consensus upon their precise limits, but they were applied with a surprising consistency. Some historians have argued that the South, as a section conscious of its own identity and interests clearly distinguishable from the North, emerged by the end of the Revolutionary era. When the Treaty of Paris was signed in 1783, New Englanders received the coveted fishing arrangements, but Southerners did not obtain the right to navigate the lower portion of the Mississippi River which ran through Spanish territory. Not until the Louisiana Purchase in 1803 were Southerners permitted to navigate and to deposit goods at New Orleans. New Englanders were never enthusiastic about the South's attempts toward transportation and deposit rights, and acrimonious debate erupted in Congress from time to time.

Washington, the Federal City

The location of the nation's permanent capital also generated sectional heat in the Confederation Congress. Each delegate hoped to have the capital as near as possible to his state. It was moved from Philadelphia to New York in 1785 when southern delegates voted with others to move it there, because they could reach New York by water more easily than Trenton, New Jersey, and Annapolis, Maryland, the cities which had been designated to serve alternately as the nation's capital. A later dispute between northern and southern states on this question ended in the famous compromise of 1790, by which the Potomac shore was selected as the site of the Federal City. Jeffersonians supported the passage of Alexander Hamilton's bill favored by the North, which authorized federal assumption of war debts incurred by the states, and Hamilton's followers in return voted to locate the government capital on the Potomac. Thomas Jefferson, then Secretary of State, negotiated for an ambitious plan of a ten-mile-square diamond laid out on a north-south axis with the town of

180

Alexandria at the southern tip. The Federal City was soon known as "Washington," and the ten-mile-square as "The District of Columbia."

The plan of the city was undertaken by Pierre Charles L'Enfant, whom Washington had known in the Revolutionary days as a member of the Corps of Engineers. In laying out the streets, L'Enfant drew on the magnificence remembered from the Versailles of his boyhood, but his hand as a city planner was guided by Jefferson, who urged wider avenues and broader vistas—a city that would make a resounding statement about the nation's intentions. The Federal City was to evoke the Greek love of beauty and the republican simplicity of Augustan Rome.

Washington was a monument to expectations. L'Enfant's plan was imaginative and ambitious, designed on balance and openness. Each branch of government was separate, in accordance with the Constitution, and was to occupy it's own enclave. Connecting those branches were broad avenues that cut diagonally across the grid of numbered and lettered streets. L'Enfant urged that the public buildings be built in the style of Greek and Roman temples—logical, rational, and functional—and insisted that the entire city should be brick or stone—structures of permanence. On paper, the design was a perfect construct of rationality and good sense; in reality, L'Enfant's grand design remained a paper dream because there was no central authority to implement it. L'Enfant was dismissed a few years after the construction began, the victim of his own stubbornness. Not particularly helpful to his cause was the demolition of a house owned by one of the District's three Commissioners that lay in the path of a street proposed on his plan.

Subsequently, Jefferson persuaded President Washington to initiate a design competition for the Capitol and the President's House. The entrants turned to architectural pattern books that had traditionally helped the carpenter-builder achieve architecture, along with more recent classical authorities, such as Stuart and Revett's *The Antiquities of Athens* (1762), one of the numerous volumes of scientific archaeology published in the late eighteenth century that provided a basis for challenging Palladian orthodoxy and stimulated an imitation of archaeological styles. The prize for the President's House was awarded, in July 1792, to the Irish-born architect James Hoban, who was also engaged to supervise construction. The Capitol competition dragged on through a year of controversy and was finally awarded to Dr. William Thornton in April 1793; to appease the second-place Stephen Hallet, the Commissioners allowed him to supervise construction. The cornerstone of the Capitol was laid by Washington in a grand Masonic ceremony in September 1793.

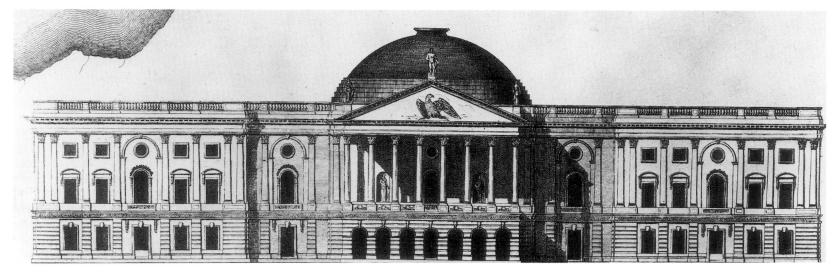

East Front of the Capitol of the United States, by William Thornton.
LIBRARY OF CONGRESS

Not everyone was pleased with the results of the competitions for a design idea, and there were open and lively exchanges and critical salvos between the competing architects of building designs. Architect George Hatfield, for instance, noted that the Capitol competition occurred "at a period when scarcely a professional architect was to be found in any of the United States; which is plainly to be seen in the pile of trash presented as designs for said building." Benjamin Latrobe did not like Hoban's President's House, finding the south entrance "disproportioned" and the north entrance "undistinguished." He would amend Hoban's design when Jefferson was in residence as president, adding the now familiar south portico that today overlooks the Ellipse. Latrobe's close connection with Thomas Jefferson was the foundation of his government practice as well as a point of departure for his running battle with William Thornton, a Federalist adherent, over Latrobe's revisions in the good doctor's Capitol design, which eventually resulted in a libel suit against Thornton, which Latrobe won. After continuous difficulties and preoccupied by the impending war in 1812 (and during which the British set the Capitol and other buildings on fire in 1814), Congress postponed further Capitol construction

182

and took the occasion to dismiss Latrobe. In 1815, however, he was recalled to repair the damage the British had done and to redesign the two wings and plan the rotunda. He was again forced out in 1817, and the first edition of the Capitol was finally completed by Charles Bulfinch in 1828. From his seclusion at Monticello, Thomas Jefferson wrote Latrobe in 1812 that the Capitol was "the first temple dedicated to the sovereignty of the people, embellishing with Athenian taste the course of a nation looking far beyond the range of Athenian destinies." Latrobe had written Jefferson, "My principles of good taste are rigid in Grecian architecture. I am a bigoted Greek in the condemnation of the Roman architecture." The neoclassical designs of the President's House and the Capitol responded to the increasing scale and aspirations of society's needs and symbolically offset the immediate realities of an undeveloped wilderness, a national government of only 130 employees, and a small army and navy.

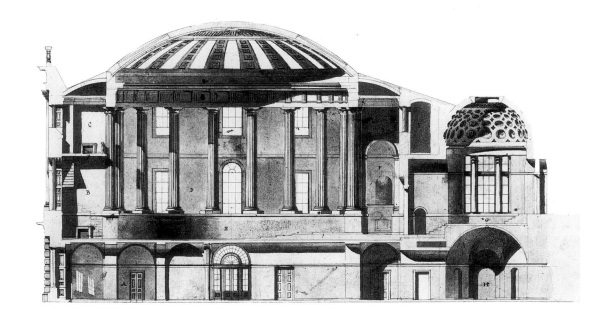

South Wing of the Capitol of the United States, by Benjamin Henry Latrobe.
LIBRARY OF CONGRESS

In its intent, its design, and its unfinished chaos, Washington symbolized the new nation. Just as L'Enfant wished to bring classical grandeur to formless woods, those who framed the Constitution hoped to impose a model republic and a stable democracy on a raw wilderness. In reality, the republic existed as an almost ungovernable collection of diverse elements caught up in an atmosphere of rapid and unpredictable change.

Differences of heritage, of culture, of occupation fragmented the new nation into regional groupings of pluralistic and diversified states. While Americans longed for stability and predictability, they lived in a world of change that was at odds with their ideal. The result was a society of contrasts, a people of paradox—crude and civilized, violent and peaceful, exuberant and restrained. "The American nation," observed a Scottish traveler, "is in a sort of middle state between barbarism and refinement." The transient legislators in the Congress deliberated in the magnificent Capitol (the British officer who was ordered to destroy it during the War of 1812 reportedly said it was "a pity to burn anything so beautiful") but lived in forced intimacy in shabby boardinghouses around Capitol Hill. The new Capitol and the President's House (which Abigail Adams concluded was "built for ages to come"), rising on opposite shores of a humid swamp, resembled ruins more than a brave new world. Between their hilltop sites was a landscape of marshes, barren knolls, tree stumps, and rubbish heaps. To this desolate spot, which concentrated the summer heat and impeded the movement of air, came the new legislators and their families to conduct the gritty business of government. According to Margaret Bayard Smith's vivacious reminiscences, the most admirable features of the landscape at the moment were the figures in it: "Never were there a plainer set of men, and I think I may add a more virtuous and enlightened one, than at present forms our administration." But, of course, the cheerful Mrs. Smith, wife of the editor of the administration paper *The National Intelligencer,* had a house of her own.

North Wing of the Capitol, watercolor by William Birch, 1800.
LIBRARY OF CONGRESS

Yet the dream of a planned monument to republicanism persisted, and L'Enfant's plan remained in the first decades only a statement of intention. When Abigail Adams arrived from Boston to join her husband, nothing in the letters she had received had prepared her for what she found. Washington was a mix of woods and swamp—"romantic," she thought, "but a wild wilderness at present." Alexandria, across the river, was tolerable, but Georgetown to the north was "the very dirtyest Hole I ever saw." The President and the First Lady shivered in the autumn damp because although wood was plentiful, "people cannot be found to cut and cart it." The executive mansion was especially jarring: only one wing had been completed, the main stairs had not been built, and Mrs. Adams had to hang laundry in the East Room. Until 1834 there were only two major federal buildings—the Capitol and the White House (so named after workmen slapped white paint over the smoke-stained presidential residence in 1814)—and four minor ones. "I was delighted with the whole aspect of Washington," reported Frances Trollope in 1832:

It has been laughed at by foreigners, and even by natives, because the original plan of the city was upon an enormous scale, and but a very small part of it has been as yet executed. But I confess I see nothing in the least degree ridiculous about it; the original design, which was as beautiful as it was extensive, has been in no way departed from, and all that has been done has been done well.

The growth of the city was agonizingly slow. It was "called the City of Magnificent Distances, but it might with greater propriety be termed the City of Magnificent Intentions," wrote Charles Dickens in 1842:

Spacious avenues, that begin in nothing, and lead nowhere; streets, mile-long, that only want houses, roads and inhabitants; Public buildings that need but a public to be complete; and ornaments of great thoroughfares, which only lack great thoroughfares to ornament—are its leading features. One might fancy the season over, and most of the houses gone out of town for ever with their masters. . . . Such as it is it is likely to remain.

The arts and sciences flourished in Washington during Jefferson's eight years as third President of the United States. Benjamin Henry Latrobe, Jefferson's protégé and appointee as Surveyor of Public Buildings, exerted significant influence for more than a decade designing and supervising work on both the Capitol and the

President's House. He had by 1803 a national reputation as both an architect and engineer, with the Philadelphia city waterworks and the Greek Revival Bank of Pennsylvania to his credit. His professional skills covered the range of building design, and his career in federal architecture was a strong mixture of aesthetic sophistication and technical innovation. Even though his close connection with Jefferson was the basis of his government practice, his relationship with his patron faltered in a battle over the ceiling in the House of Representatives. Latrobe insisted that Jefferson's academically classical solution would leak. A compromise solution did leak, and the matter did not rest until Latrobe rebuilt the ceiling his way after the fire of 1814. Preoccupied by the war, Congress postponed further construction on the Capitol. Dismissed in early 1812, Latrobe was recalled in 1815 to repair the damage the British had done. He redesigned the two wings, planned the central or rotunda section, and rebuilt a large part of the wings. In 1817 he was forced out by an aggressive District of Columbia Commissioner, an aloof President Monroe, and a suspicious Congress. Charles Bulfinch arrived to replace him in 1818. "Government service," he lamented with reason, "is a ruinous connection." Although there have been subsequent changes in its appearance, notably a higher central dome of cast iron completed in 1865, the Capitol as we know it today is largely Latrobe's building.

View of the Capitol, by Charles Burton, 1824.
THE METROPOLITAN MUSEUM OF ART. PURCHASE, JOSEPH PULITZER BEQUEST

The Greek Revival

As Jefferson's idealistic adaptation of a Roman temple for the state capitol in Richmond, Virginia—copied from the Maison Carrée in Nîmes, France—marked the beginning of a Roman phase in American neoclassicism, William Strickland's design for the Second Bank of the United States (1817–24) in Philadelphia more than a quarter of a century later signaled the turn toward Greece as the dominant inspiration for public buildings. Strickland, who trained under Latrobe, had suggested that the Parthenon was the right classical model because the ancient building had also housed the public treasure. The Second Bank, a federally chartered private institution, was established in 1816 and popularly viewed as public property. Its Greek Revival architectural style, like its economic precepts, symbolized stability and order and was part of the search for a national identity in a period of rapidly expanding trade and commerce. Having secured a nation, Americans were turning their energies to securing a continent. Nicholas Biddle, who believed that "the two great truths in the world are the Bible and Grecian architecture," was appointed one of the directors and later became president of the Second Bank. His preferences for the Greek classical style as well as for cautious public expenditure were clearly expressed in his guidelines for the design competition: "We seek a chaste imitation of Grecian architecture in its simplest and least expensive form." Biddle was a major protagonist as well as a victim of the bitter conflicts involved in the young nation's economic development. Toward the end of the Bank's charter in 1832, President Andrew Jackson led a successful campaign to destroy Biddle's system, but not before the Second Bank had scattered twenty-six "money temples" around the country, all designed in the Greek Revival style that was fast becoming synonymous with banking.

The Greek Revival was the first pervasive and self-conscious nationalistic movement in American architecture. Strickland and a contemporary, Robert Mills, who had been a fellow assistant in Latrobe's office, were proponents of a strict adherence to the proportions and character of the Greek orders and Greek ornamental system with deliberate authenticity in a drive for archaeological correctness. The increasing body of specific knowledge about Greek buildings themselves was made available to this generation of American architects through pattern books and archaeological works published abroad, as well as builders' handbooks published in this country—the most important ones written by Asher Benjamin and Minard Lafever—which carried the basic information about the Greek orders and Greek ornamental detail. Strickland's Second Bank was the first public building in America to be based on the Parthenon and was taken from the restored façade of that ancient building as illustrated in Stuart and Revett's *The Antiquities of Athens.* Poised, rhythmic, and absolute, the proportions and details of the Doric order in this temple front and entablature are closer to the Greek than anything built in this country up to that time, giving the building the distinction of being the first truly Greek Revival building in America. And so the temple took its place in the American scene. When the grandiose Girard College was planned, Nicholas Biddle, as a board member, was determined to see the new buildings cast in the image of Greece and engaged Thomas U. Walter as the architect. The principal building, now Founder's Hall, is a large Corinthian temple, built between 1833 and 1847.

Walter used the pure temple form on other occasions and for different purposes. One, because of its location, is of particular interest. In 1835, the Hibernian Society of Charleston, South Carolina, a social and charitable group, held a design competition that Walter won. His project for Hibernian Hall (1839–40) is a pure Ionic temple with an order based largely on that of the Erectheum on the Acropolis. Although Charleston is highly regarded today for its eighteenth-century colonial architecture, large portions of the city were destroyed by several disastrous fires (most notably the devastating conflagrations of 1740, 1778, 1796, and 1838). Except for a few significant clusters of important colonial remains, the major architectural character of the city was determined in the early nineteenth century in the Greek Revival style. Of the many churches built there during this era, seven are of the pure Greek temple type—five Doric and two Corinthian—as is Strickland's College of Charleston (1828–29).

Robert Mills

The prevalence of wood as a building material posed the constant menace of fire, and from early times builders searched for better means of controlling it. There had been experiments with brick in Boston and metal in England, but the interior framing of masonry walls contributed little toward reducing the risk. Not until Latrobe introduced sophisticated techniques of vaulting in an addition to the old Treasury Building in Washington, which he designed in 1805, were Americans able to think in terms of fireproof construction. The first building in America conceived with fireproof construction was Robert Mills's Record Office (known today as the "Fireproof Building"), built in Charleston between 1822 and 1827. Early in 1820, after a short period in Baltimore, Mills had moved to Charleston after "receiving the appointment of Engineer and Architect of the State, and a commission seat on the Board of Commissioners of Public Works." South Carolina was a leading producer of cotton and as the rich lands of Alabama and Mississippi began to yield their crops, there was a theory that Charleston might be the port for the staple if the transportation problem could be solved. Mills was ordered to design a line of waterways and roads from the Cooper River across the continent to the Columbia River, with Charleston as the entrance—a grand scheme that could not be realized.

It was in his capacity as "Architect of the State" that he was commissioned to design a fireproof record office for South Carolina, which is recognized today as one of the most innovative buildings of the first half of the nineteenth century. The program of the Fireproof Building commission simply called for office and record-storage spaces, planned in an efficient and secure manner. Mills's solution was correspondingly straightforward. The building is a two-story rectangular block set on a high basement; in the center of each of the long sides is a colossal Greek Doric portico with four columns and a pediment. The main massing is staunchly neoclassical in its plainness and dignified in its use of Greek-inspired motifs. But the importance of the building lies not in the outward simplicity of its style and tradition, but in its fireproof function and structural necessity. Mills's governing objective was to make the building fireproof. The only way to accomplish this was to build entirely in masonry, and this was precisely what he did. He used the vault for fire prevention to create cellular spaces of groin-vaulted modules repeated end to end, these clusters separated by barrel-vaulted corridors. No timber was used except for the ceilings of the third floor and the roof structure. The Fireproof Building in Charleston was the climax of Mills's early career; its success showed him to be a master of his profession, with a practical yet refined sense of architectural form and a supreme command of structure. Mills produced a quality and kind of construction that was unique and unmatched by any other building in America in his day, except for the works of Latrobe. In 1830 he returned to Washington to take up his duties as architect for the federal government.

When Mills arrived, the Capitol and the President's House were complete. In addition there were four office buildings occupied by the several departments of the executive branch of the government simply designed in a conservative neoclassical style. Otherwise the city offered only a handful of elegant houses scattered among straggling rows of shanties, boardinghouses, and hotels—the rest was muddy dirt tracks and unkempt open fields. By the time he left office (a position he described as "Architect of Public Buildings") in 1851, he had added to official Washington three imposing Greek Revival structures—the Patent Office, the Treasury Building, and the Post Office Building. In addition, he gave the city its finest tribute to a national hero, the soaring obelisk of the Washington Monument. Of the three government structures, the Treasury Building was the most important and the most controversial of Mills's career. Located on Fifteenth Street, between the converging lines of Pennsylvania and New York avenues, it was the first major departure from the L'Enfant plan, interrupting as it did the grand vista from the White House to the Capitol. This location has been a source of violent controversy ever since the building was originally conceived. Mills proposed to site the building fifty feet back from Fifteenth Street, out of respect for L'Enfant's plan, but legend has it that President Jackson himself, wishing to end the dispute, walked to the site and, pointing his cane, said, "Build it here!" As described by Mills in 1847, it was a building "extending 336 feet with a depth in the center . . . of 190 feet. Each floor contains forty-nine apartments, or in the three stories above the basement, 135 rooms." Begun in 1836, the Treasury Department Building took thirty-three years to complete. Its superb colonnade is composed of seventy-four granite columns, brought by ship from Maine; thirteen teams of horses and oxen were required to move each one into place to be raised into position.

The basic problems that confronted Mills in planning the Treasury Building were identical to those of the Fireproof Building in Charleston: to provide efficiently arranged office spaces and to make the building fireproof. His solution was essentially the same—he developed opposing ranges of groin-vaulted office cells separated by barrel-vaulted interior corridors. The magnitude of the Treasury Building far exceeded anything Mills had ever attempted, but the flexibility of his structural system made it possible for him to achieve as

190

many spaces as necessary. The interior represents Mills at his finest: it is clean and strong, but it is also dynamically graceful, an effect accomplished without a single conceit through the simplest possible means. Efficiently planned within a particularly American context and boldly executed with extraordinary qualities of geometric simplicity and revealed architecture, Mills's Treasury Building represents the most rationally conceived building yet designed by an American-born architect in the Greek Revival mode. Because of its simplicity, strength, and honesty, the Treasury Building brought to Washington a freshness and vitality more in tune with the aggressive national temperament than the staid dignity of the President's House and the Capitol.

By the time that Robert Mills left office in 1851, the Greek Revival style had permeated from the high style through popular culture to the folk level of American architecture. Adopted by the common man as well as the professional architect, it became the first style in American history to be consciously understood and embraced as a truly national style of building. Henry Adams in 1850, speaking of himself in the third person as was his wont, said of Mills's buildings:

Venturing outside into the air reeking with the thick odor of the catalpa trees, he found himself on an earth-road, or village street, with wheel-tracks meandering from the colonnade of the Treasury hard by, to the white marble columns and fronts of the Post Office and Patent Office which faced each other in the distance, like white Greek temples in the abandoned gravel-pits of a deserted Syrian city.

This was a period in which the federal presence was expressed in stone and mortar in the prevailing classical imperative. Urban custom houses, like banks, located even far from the capital center of the nation, provided the full temple ambience and spoke in the classical tongue about federal authority—unabashedly of the government's dignity and optimistically of its reliability and permanence.

Latrobe in New Orleans

A law of 1807 appropriated funds for "a good and sufficient house" for customs collection in New Orleans, and Albert Gallatin, the Swiss-born genius then serving as Secretary of the Treasury, gave the commission to Latrobe. This was the first allocation for construction of the type of building that would later become part of the Treasury Department's "public building program": custom houses, courthouses, and post offices. Latrobe sent his completed designs to Gallatin in late April 1807 along with a cost estimate and the interesting news that Robert Alexander, who had been one of the contractors for Latrobe's Washington Navy Yard work, was planning to move to New Orleans to open a building business and would be willing to take the contract. The job was rushed: all of the bricks were made and the joinery done in Philadelphia. The contractor purchased a brig there, loading her with bricks and joinery; on the way to New Orleans she stopped at Alexandria to pick up all the ironwork and manufactured parts that had been made in the Washington area. Alexander arrived in May 1808, and the building was completed a year later. This was an ambitious project to be undertaken at a modest cost. The lower floor, for stored goods, was covered with fireproof brick vaults. Above it rose walls faced with Philadelphia brick; the main front had a recessed loggia with two Greek Doric stone columns *in antis,* and there was a wood-shingled hipped roof. In refusing to follow the New Orleans custom of building all walls on logs laid in the foundation trenches, Latrobe made a serious error. His masonry footings produced fragmentary and unequal settling, resulting in serious cracks. By 1817 the building was an unusable ruin, and a new custom house by a local architect was erected to replace it—a bitter disappointment to Latrobe and to the city.

In early winter 1818, Latrobe himself took ship for New Orleans. His designs for the New Orleans waterworks, custom house, and lighthouse for the mouth of the Mississippi had given him familiarity with the conditions there, and correspondence with Robert Alexander had provided further insight. He knew that New Orleans was the growing mecca of restless Americans and restless American dollars and that its prospects for the future were brighter than those of any other American city at that time.

Romantic New Orleans, picturesque New Orleans, carefree New Orleans—there lay the shores of illusion, the Crescent City, the big river's end. Its location put the city in a position to exact commercial tribute from almost the entire region between the Appalachians and the Rocky Mountains, as long as water was the most practical means of transporting goods in bulk. Rafts, barges, flatboats, and keelboats were used on the Mississippi almost from the time the first Anglo-American settlers crossed the Appalachians, and such craft continued to bring produce to New Orleans throughout the antebellum years. Before steamboat traffic began in 1812, downstream from Pittsburgh took six weeks; upstream, if it could be done at all, took seventeen weeks or more. In 1814 Captain Henry Miller Shreve brought the steam-driven *Enterprise* down from Pittsburgh, and it huffed and puffed its way back to Louisville from New Orleans in twenty-five days. The river steamboat gave the first impetus to western growth, by making upriver trade possible and greatly reducing transportation costs, particularly in the export of cotton, timber, metals, sugar, and grains. Great skill was needed to navigate these western rivers with their fluctuations in depth, their ledges, rocks, sandbars, and worst of all, their snags. The captains who survived were indeed skillful men, as every reader of Mark Twain recalls, who knew every inch of the waters they navigated. The boast of some Mississippi River captains that they could carry a heavy cargo and navigate in heavy dew because their draft was so shallow was doubtless exaggeration, but there is evidence they could manage in water of only twenty-two inches in depth.

When Latrobe arrived in the booming New Orleans of 1819—a sort of separate, independent, sun-soaked principality—he was enthralled with his new environment, the new sights, the new sounds, the new ways of living, the city's gaiety. Henry Bradshaw Fearon, an advance agent for immigrants, who arrived in New Orleans on a Sunday also in 1819, could hardly get over his surprise at finding on a Sabbath in the United States the markets, shops, theaters, taverns, gambling-houses, and public ballrooms open. "The French language is still predominant in New Orleans," he observed.

The population is said to be 30,000, two-thirds of which do not speak English. I find that the general manners and habits of New Orleans are very relaxed. . . . The general style of living is luxurious. Houses are elegantly furnished . . . the ladies dress with expensive elegance. The sources of public amusement are numerous and varied. . . . to all men who desire only to live a short life but a merry one, I have no hesitation in recommending New Orleans.

For Latrobe here was a new kind of America to study. New Orleans was a symbol of the inclusiveness of the young country, for there were gathered in close interaction the three peoples who had played a chief part in settling the American continent—the English, the French, and the Spanish. The growing wealth of this southern metropolis, particularly from its cotton and sugar, also brought settlers and adventurers from

Scotland, England, and Germany. New Orleans was the American melting pot as no other city in the country could have been.

Founded as a trading post, one hundred and ten miles from the multiple mouths of the Mississippi River, by the French in 1718, New Orleans remained under French rule until 1763. It was a planned town, laid out on a grid along the river, with the Place d'Armes (now Jackson Square), surrounded by a church, school, and governor's palace, forming the heart of the Vieux Carré. France ceded Louisiana to Spain, and it remained a Spanish possession for thirty-eight years, during which time Spanish law was substituted for French. The Superior Council was abolished and the *Cabildo,* or town council, created to replace it, and General Alejandro O'Reilly ordered that a suitable building be erected for its deliberations. Among the public buildings surviving today is the *Cabildo* built in 1795. This rather academic, classicizing Baroque stone edifice (except for its mansard roof added in the 1850s) is an excellent example of Spanish official colonial architecture. O'Reilly divided Louisiana into twenty-one ecclesiastical parishes, which were later to become the basis of political subdivision. Probably the most striking feature of the Spanish period in Louisiana history was the tremendous increase in population. There were about 7,500 people in the colony in 1763; by 1803 the number had grown to approximately 50,000. Most of the growth came through immigration, Arcadians being the most numerous. Heads of families were entitled to 350 to 475 yards of frontage along a river or bayou with land tracts extending back from a stream as much as a mile and a half. Because the streams run in loops and curves, lines drawn back from the water led to strangely shaped landholdings—wedge-shaped blocks and pie-shaped tracts fronting the streams—while back in the swamps are the regular, square sections of the United States land survey according to the Land Ordinance of 1785.

Louisiana was a French-speaking colony when the nineteenth century opened. In the late 1790s Napoleon Bonaparte came to power in France, and the Spanish government quickly became a puppet manipulated by the French dictator. One of Bonaparte's ambitions was to restore France's empire in the New World, so by the secret Treaty of San Ildefonso of 1800, Spain ceded Louisiana to France. Secret agreements between nations seldom remain secret for long, and Jefferson learned of the arrangement soon after he became president. He wrote that whatever power held New Orleans was the "natural and habitual enemy" of the United States, adding, "The day that France takes possession of New Orleans . . . we must marry ourselves to the British fleet and nation." While the French never succeeded in taking possession of New Orleans, except in a formal sense and even then only for the briefest of periods, a new danger threatened the United States in 1802 when the Spanish intendant in New Orleans, Juan Ventura Morales, suspended the privilege of depositing American produce at New Orleans for trans-shipment to foreign parts. The intendant acted on direct orders from Madrid, but was required by the same orders to make the cloture appear to be his own decision. Harassed and hindered American traders thought it outrageous. Perhaps royal Spanish pride moved the Spaniards to exit from the Louisiana stage with a finale which they thought might embarrass Bonaparte. The British were actively meddling in the Louisiana business by offering cash rewards to the willing Joseph Bonaparte and Talleyrand to block the sale of Louisiana in order to entangle Napoleon more deeply in colonialism, so that he could not take time for more warfare in Europe. Napoleon's decision to sell the whole of his Louisiana province came suddenly. The peace that then temporarily blessed Europe was distasteful to him; he wished to get back to the glorious drums and trumpets of war. Louisiana had become a bore. Here was the chance to get money, to rid himself of the American problem, and to get back to his dream of reshaping Europe with power, ball, and bayonet: hence his offer.

The Louisiana Purchase

With a few strokes of the pen, the continental domain of the United States was more than doubled in April 1803 when Jefferson purchased the Great Plains from Napoleon Bonaparte—the so-called Louisiana Purchase—for $15 million. The United States was now in the possession of the heartland of the continent and had gained a position of potential independence from European powers. Jefferson's purchase of Louisiana was a triumph of diplomatic skill, a startling idea that could only have arisen in a nation and with an administration determined to settle international disputes without resorting to force. The great man from Monticello saw in this arrangement the birth of nothing less than an "Empire for Liberty"—an asylum for mankind that was intended to hold sway in the world not by arms or political power but by the sheer majesty of ideas and ideals. His vision was of an agrarian utopia stretching out to the Rockies; to Andrew Jackson he wrote in September 1803, "the world will see here such an extent of country under a free and moderate government as it has never yet seen." Thomas Jefferson had done a great deed. "I stretched the Constitution until it cracked," he told Congress, "yet the fertility of the country, its climate and extent, all promise in due season important aids to our treasury." The purchase of Louisiana is now regarded as the chief constructive act of his presidency; in his *History of the United States,* Henry Adams concluded it was an event that ranks in importance below only the achievements of independence and union. The great republican experiment would be an example and a beacon, unsheltered and unafraid of the light of truth. To James Madison, Jefferson wrote in 1809: "I am persuaded that no better constitution was ever before so well calculated as ours for extensive empire and self-government."

The Louisiana Purchase was probably the best real estate deal in all history, but the treaty of cession was vague as to boundaries. What passed from France to the United States was what France had received from Spain—and France, wrote Charles Gravier, the Comte de Vergennes, French foreign minister, could take possession of nothing except "between the right [west] bank of the Mississippi and New Mexico." No boundaries, save near New Orleans and along the Mississippi, were known precisely. When Robert Livingston and James Monroe attempted to discover the exact nature of their bargain, they could get no more from Talleyrand than the cryptic remark: "I can give you no direction; you have made a noble bargain for yourselves and I suppose you will make the most of it." The standard American argument was that the Purchase extended at least as far to the southwest as the Rio Grande; but Monroe (with Madison's connivance) had been prepared to retreat in 1815 to the Colorado River in Texas or even the Sabine as the southwestern boundary, and extending from the Gulf to an undetermined Canadian boundary in the north.

The Federalists bitterly denounced this purchase of a "wilderness." Tracing the uncertain borders of the suddenly expanded nation occupied a large part of the attention and energies of young people in love with their West—and much of that energy was spent on the perplexing question of the American claim that West Florida was part of Louisiana. West of the Mississippi the moribund, neglected province of Texas slept in the sun and the Louisiana-Texas border became a squall line between contending cultures. The disputed area became neutral ground—a haven for horse thieves and other outlaws—until the western boundary was finally fixed at the Sabine River by the Adams-Onís Treaty of 1819. To the east, the United States claimed the area between the Mississippi and Perdido rivers (West Florida) from the time of the Louisiana Purchase. The census of 1810 showed that the Territory of Orleans (the present state of Louisiana), not including West Florida, had a population of more than 76,000 people. In April 1812 Louisiana became the eighteenth state of the Union, over the objections of Josiah Quincy of Massachusetts, who asserted that Congress had no right to extend the rights of citizenship to "a hotch-pot with the wild men on the Missouri, nor with the mixed, though more respectable race of Anglo-Hispanic-Gallo-Americans who bask on the sands at the mouth of the Mississippi." The drain of population from the older southern states to the settlement into the undeveloped sections of the southwest and the rapid advance of the Cotton Kingdom was registered in the admission of other new states into the Union following Louisiana: Mississippi, 1817; Alabama, 1819; Missouri, 1821; Arkansas, 1836; Florida and Texas, 1845. By 1830 the Gulf states had surpassed the Atlantic seaboard states in the production of cotton.

When Latrobe came to New Orleans in January 1819 to expedite the completion of the waterworks, the Crescent City was the greatest port and largest city in the South. Latrobe's twenty-three years in America had made him keenly aware of the crosscurrents that eddied through American life, and the observations in his journals and sketches give a graphic picture of the appearances and sounds of New Orleans, the shock of two opposing cultures—in the markets, the streets, the hotels and taverns, at the balls and theaters. Latrobe was especially interested in the "growing Americanism of this city," the gradual changes in New Orleans life which the influx of Americans was bringing about, and tartly observed that the Yankees were acting more like conquerors than newly arrived citizens. "What is good and bad in the French manners, and opinions must give way, and the American notions of right and wrong, of convenience and inconvenience will take their place," he maintained. But he concluded with enlightened skepticism, "When this period arrives, it would be folly to say that things are better or worse than they now are." He observed the worldly manner in which the French Sunday was kept in "the Southern Babylon" and noted that the Protestant clergy were united in attacking the

Creole view that after attending Mass, the rest of the day should be considered a holiday. Soon, he suspected, "Sunday will become as gloomy and ennuyant as elsewhere among us." He noted a similar development in the architecture and building ways of American merchants:

They have already begun to introduce the detestable, lop-sided, London house, in which a common passage and stairs acts as a common sewer to all the necessities of the dwelling . . . the American suburb, already exhibits the flat [red-brick front], dingy character of Market Street, in Philadelphia . . . instead of the motley and picturesque effect of the stuccoed French buildings of the city. We shall introduce many grand and profitable improvements, but they will take the place of much elegance, ease, and some convenience.

In fact, the French Creole regional character of domestic architecture of New Orleans had more tenacity than Latrobe expected, and its building types spread upriver. The soil, the climate, and the general pace of life soon convinced the newly arrived Americans that mere copying of the plans and appearance of northern homes was inappropriate, and gradually a new vernacular architectural style developed, entirely regional in its character and in surprising harmony with the earlier French structures. Frontier houses were usually one story in height, containing a row of rooms, with chimneys in the center or at the ends, the whole surrounded by a railed porch, which offered access to the rooms. A steeply pitched hip roof covered the house proper and swept out at a lower angle to be supported by slender posts on the porch. Tyrone Power, the Irish actor, during his travels in the Gulf states in 1835 was impressed by the restless energy and acquisitive spirit of the recent settlers:

These frontier tamers of the swamp and forest are hardy, indefatigable and enterprising to a degree; despising and condemning luxury and refinement, courting labour, and even making a pride of the privation, which they . . . continue to endure with their families. . . . Their pride does not consist in fine houses, fine raiment, costly services of plate or refined cookery; they live in humble dwellings of wood, wear the coarsest habits, and live on the plainest fare.

Opposite
Spiral stair at Houmas Plantation, built on land once occupied by Houmas Indians, built in 1840 by General Wade Hampton for his daughter and son-in-law, John Smith Preston. Though the architect is unknown, it seems likely that Preston, a patron of the arts and one of the men who helped finance the sculptor Hiram Powers's trip to Italy, had something to do with matters of the design.

The plantation houses in the lower parishes of Louisiana were larger, mostly two stories in height, the lower of stucco-covered brick, the upper of wood. They had much in common with the frontier type and may have evolved from the "raised cottages" along the river bottoms, built on stilts to avoid flooding. George Washington Cable in *Old Creole Days* (1879) managed to capture the flavor of "an old colonial plantation-house half in ruin" in the Creole Delta:

It stood aloof from civilization, the tracts that had once been its indigo fields given over to their first noxious wildness. . . . The house was of heavy cypress, lifted up on pillars, grim, solid, and spiritless, its massive build a strong reminder of days still earlier, when every man had been his own peace officer and the insurrection of the blacks a daily contingency. Its dark, weather-beaten roof and sides were hoisted up above the jungly plain in a distracted way. . . . Around it was a dense growth of low water willows, with half a hundred sorts of thorny or fetid bushes.

Behind the legend of the Greek Revival plantation mansion with its slave quarter behind stretched the reality of violence and crudity, of the practical affairs of money, crops, weather, the management of labor, disease, debts, gossip, and petty frustrations interspersed with the simple pleasures of camp meetings, courtship, love, marriage, children, visiting, and hunting and fishing. Moreover, the serenity of the big mansion was to be troubled, and a great shadow cast on southern lives by the approaching storm over slavery, which most thoughtful men foresaw.

As the winter of 1819 wore into spring, Latrobe's architectural business in New Orleans expanded. He completed the waterworks and inspected the Mississippi lighthouse, for which he had made the original design in 1805–06, to review the work and make recommendations to correct its bad cracks from unequal settlement. In May he was commissioned to design the central façade tower of the Cathedral. He received the job, as noted in the council action, because "the steeple represented on his drawings harmonizes perfectly with the kind of architecture according to which the parish church was built." This to him was a welcome vindication of his architectural taste and tact. The Cathedral tower, he believed, was but the beginning of a busy practice which the growth of the city would give him. In late September he took passage north on the brig *Emma* for New York to close out his affairs in Philadelphia and Baltimore, visiting friends and relatives before returning with his family in the late winter. They traveled overland to Wheeling to board the steamboat

Columbus down the Ohio and Mississippi. The whole trip was a succession of mechanical failures and tortuous delays—what should have been an eight-day voyage lengthened into five weeks—and the Latrobe family finally arrived in New Orleans in early April 1820. They spent one day en route on the bluff of the river in the town of Natchez where imposing Greek Revival mansions were rising one after the other for the cotton planters. In one of the finest, now known as Auburn, designed in 1812 by the New Englander Levi Weeks, lived a Mrs. Harding, an old friend of the Latrobes'. Auburn would be occupied in the late 1850s by Stephen Duncan, a banker and one of the greatest cotton planters of the lower South, who owned eight absentee plantations on the rich soils in Concordia Parish, Louisiana, across the river from Natchez, with 1,018 plantation slaves and 23 house servants, and produced 4,000 bales of cotton annually. The proprietors of these plantations, arable lands which travelers on Mississippi steamboats reported were as "level as a billiard table," were monopolists who had acquired wealth from their exploitation of slave labor. According to the New Orleans *Crescent* they exercised "the authority of ownership over estates as broad as some German principalities, and yielding far greater revenues. But very few of these lords of the soil reside on their estates but have their residence across the river in Natchez or elsewhere."

The Latrobes returned to a crowd of people in New Orleans who eagerly awaited their arrival as the *Columbus* made fast and joined a long parade of flatboats moored five or six tiers deep at the levee, a broad dike of earth along the Mississippi where the produce of the upper Mississippi and Ohio valleys was deposited. Mrs. Latrobe, who had feared that New Orleans would be "a vile hole" like the filthy and wicked confusion of grog shops and gambling halls of the riverside area of Natchez "under the hill," was agreeably surprised by the quality of it all—oranges for sale, vegetables in the market, the old Spanish houses, the Ursuline Convent, and the Place d'Armes. The New Orleans venture was beginning auspiciously with the waterworks nearing completion and the Cathedral tower almost finished. Another architectural commission came in from the Louisiana State Bank. As the summer advanced, the level of the Mississippi fell, and yellow fever broke out and spread its deadly mantle over the city. And on September 3, 1820, Latrobe the brilliant architect succumbed—one more victim of that terrible yellow-fever year—and his bereaved family returned to Baltimore to start life over anew.

Overleaf Dome of the old House Chamber, now Statuary Hall, United
States Capitol, designed by Benjamin Henry Latrobe, 1819.

East portico of Monticello, Charlottesville, Virginia, designed and built by Thomas Jefferson between 1769 and 1809. Monticello (an Italian word for "little mountain") was strictly Jefferson's own creation, and no other house in America reflects so well the personality of its owner. Appointed Minister to France in 1784, Jefferson lost no opportunity to visit the great architectural monuments of Europe. One house that he particularly admired was the Hôtel de Salm in Paris—a house of one story and a dome, which is generally considered one of the handsomest structures built during the reign of Louis XVI. "I was violently smitten with the Hôtel de Salm," Jefferson said, and returned to Monticello to raise the ceilings of the three main rooms on the first floor to a height more compatible with current French taste and to double the size of the house by adding new rooms on the east. Jefferson moved the east portico out and reduced it to a single story. Piazzas, as he called them, were then placed at the north and south ends of the building; the one adjoining his own rooms on the south end of the house was used as a workroom and greenhouse. In later years, he wrote that on his mountaintop "all my wishes end where I hope my days will end, at Monticello."

Overleaf

Parlor at Monticello. This large and elegant room in the form of a semi-octagon is west of the entrance hall and separated from it by glass doors. The ten-inch squares of the parquet floor are cherry, bordered with beechwood, following Jefferson's design. He had seen parquet floors in France and made drawings of several patterns. This is the first floor of its kind in America. Family musicales were held in this room. Jefferson hung his finest paintings on its walls; he reported forty-eight pictures here in 1809. Jefferson gave particular attention to the interior decoration and furnishings of the parlor—the symmetrical focal point of the house and its most spacious public room. The best furniture was arranged in the French style, with tables and chairs placed in conversational groupings before the fireplace or windows.

Octagonal dome over the center portion of Monticello. Jefferson erected the dome directly in the center of the house "precisely on the same principles as those of the meat market in Paris." The *Halle aux Bleds*, where he frequently met Maria Cosway, provided him with architectural and engineering ideas he took back to America. The dome's construction, in small pieces of wood, was extremely advanced for its day. In fact, the entire roof of Monticello was not easy to construct. Jefferson designed a compound roof, a combination of hips and gables, making the framing unusual and tricky, particularly for workmen in his part of Virginia. The finished floor plan under the dome was a rampant self-indulgence in octagonality: four semi-octagon rooms, two semi-octagon piazzas, a semi-octagon balcony, and a full octagon bedroom. The Marquis de Chastéllux, visiting Monticello in 1782, commented that "Mr. Jefferson is the first American who has consulted the Fine Arts to know how he should shelter himself from the weather."

Opposite

Jefferson's cabinet or study at Monticello. Of special note among the furniture original to Monticello is the revolving chair which, in conjunction with a table and the seat of a long bench, formed a sort of chaise longue. The assembled pieces enabled Jefferson to write in the half-recumbent position forced on him in later years by his rheumatic ailments. On the table is John Hawkins's and Charles Willson Peale's Patent Polygraph number 57, an instrument for simultaneously copying letters. The Marquis de Chastellux described Jefferson in 1782 as "an American, who, without ever having quitted his own country, is Musician, Draftsman, Surveyor, Astronomer, Natural Philosopher, Jurist, and Statesman, a Senator of America . . . and finally a Philosopher." Undoubtedly one of the most brilliant men of his time, Jefferson was also an unflagging correspondent and an archivally oriented record keeper. The nearly 20,000 letters he left document the astonishing breadth of his intellect and accomplishments as well as the intimacy of his relationship with an uncommonly close family. So that he might write where and when he pleased, he made use of the writing box or lap desk, shown on the leather couch.

Jefferson's bedroom at Monticello. The bed is located in an alcove between the bedroom and the adjoining study, or what he called the cabinet. The door of this apartment was seldom opened by anyone except Jefferson, for this was his *sanctum sanctorum*. When Mrs. William Thornton visited Monticello in 1802 with her husband, the architect working on the Capitol building in Washington, she recorded in her diary that she had been looking forward to browsing in Jefferson's library, for she had heard it was "one of the best private libraries on the continent." She learned what every guest at Monticello quickly discovered: the library suite was "constantly locked." Over the alcove is a small room, reached by a narrow stairway, which was Jefferson's clothes closet; three oval openings above the bed were for light and ventilation. Jefferson died in this room in this bed on July 4, 1826, at the age of eighty-three.

Rotunda of the University of Virginia, designed by Thomas Jefferson in 1821. Jefferson called the rotunda the capstone of the university. Classical forms did not merely symbolize the virtuous ideals and principles of the ancients, he believed, but they had some active power of inducing virtuous behavior. His conviction helps to explain Jefferson's enthusiasm for Roman forms as an expression of American ideals and his decision to house the University of Virginia in rows of temples oriented to a library (a Pantheon, embodiment of classical virtue and wisdom) rather than to center its campus on a Christian chapel. Jefferson adapted the Pantheon at one-half scale for the rotunda design, reintroducing the podium on which it rested before the foundation was obscured by the debris of millenia. As befits the smaller size, Jefferson used only six columns and

eliminated the extra pediment; the building, with its native red brick and white moldings, took on a distinctly American character.

Opposite

Interior of the rotunda of the University of Virginia. Within this building Jefferson designed the dome room, which was to be a library, at exactly the proportions of the Pantheon, but he used a continuous peristyle instead of a series of exedras. Below, he designed two floors of oval rooms, served by a dumbbell-shaped entrance hall, seen here.

Oatlands, Leesburg, Virginia, built in 1803 by George Carter; altered in the 1830s in the Greek Revival style. Carter was the great-grandson of Virginia's famed planter Robert "King" Carter, and he built Oatlands from bricks fired on the property and from wood brought from the surrounding forests. By 1816, Carter had constructed a gristmill on nearby Goose Creek, supplying ground flour for President Monroe's nearby Oak Hill estate and other Loudoun County farms. Soon "Oatlands Mill" became a center of a thriving community that included the miller's residence, a blacksmith shop, a school, and a store. In 1965 Oatlands, with its 261-acre estate, was presented to the National Trust for Historic Preservation.

Overleaf
First-floor bed chamber of Gunston Hall, Lorton, Virginia, built by George Mason in 1755–59 on Doeg's Neck, a peninsula in the Potomac River, and designed by William Buckland. Mason began to build his new house on lands he inherited about five years after his marriage in 1750 to Ann Eilbeck. On the land that he farmed, he cultivated tobacco, corn, and wheat. He named Gunston Hall after an ancestral home in Staffordshire, England, and signed William Buckland, an Oxford-born carpenter-joiner, to a four-year indenture to make architectural changes in the unfinished structure. Although the exact nature of Buckland's work at Gunston Hall is not fully documented, his influence is evident in the design of its elaborately carved interior. A formal parlor in the Palladian style and a Chinese-style dining room were on the west side of the house. The east rooms of the mansion were more utilitarian in purpose and less elaborate in finish. This northeast bed chamber on the first floor served not only as the Masons' bedroom, but it was truly the center of operations for the domestic management of the plantation.

215

Virginia State Capitol in Richmond, Virginia, designed by Thomas Jefferson in 1785 and completed in 1788. Modeled on the *Maison Carrée* in Nîmes, with Ionic columns (symbolic of wisdom and appropriate for a legislative building) substituted for the original's Corinthian (symbolic of beauty). Jefferson wrote that he had sat before this Roman temple in France for hours, "gazing . . . like a lover at his mistress." He sent the Virginia legislature sketches of the *Maison* to provide classical authority for his proposed design for a state capitol at Richmond. To adapt the windowless Roman temple to a legislative building, Jefferson inserted rows of windows and a gallery, which later collapsed. Explaining the choice of the Roman temple plan for the Virginia building, Jefferson wrote: "Erected in the time of the Caesars and which is allowed without contradiction to be the most perfect and precious remain of antiquity in existence. . . . I determined, therefore, to adopt this model and to have all its proportions justly drewed."

West view, or entrance façade, of Mount Vernon, which reveals the evolution of a modest farmhouse to what George Washington considered an appropriate setting for his private and public life between 1757 and his death in 1799. Self-sufficency, agrarianism, and republicanism were fundamental beliefs of Washington, and so it was logical that he turned to the classical design theories of Andrea Palladio when he began to enlarge Mount Vernon. In the 1780s, Washington adopted the new decorative style of Robert Adam, which provided a classical framework for the symbolism of the new Republic. His major architectural problem was the asymmetry of the doors and windows on the façade. Washington raised the roof to two-and-a-half stories, and the entire house was sheathed with pine boards deeply scored and rusticated with paint and sand to look like blocks of stone. The cupola, built in 1778 and repaired in 1784, not only emphasized the true center line of the building but served as a ventilator to help draw fresh air through the house.

Overleaf

Red Room, The White House, furnished as a drawing room in the Empire style. The mahogany-veneered sofa at the right was made 1815–25. The *gueridon* in front of it is labeled under the top by Charles Honoré Lannuier, New York City, 1815, and is mahogany with satinwood inlay, bronze and brass mounts, and has an inlaid marble top.

Above the sofa hangs *View of Rocky Mountains*, signed and dated 1871 by Albert Bierstadt. To its left is one of a pair of eighteenth-century gilded wooden sconces made in England for the American market. The portrait of Dolley Madison on the adjacent wall was painted by Gilbert Stuart in 1804 and is believed to have hung in this room in 1813. Below it is a Severin Roesen *Still Life with Fruit* of about 1850. Beneath the paintings is one of a pair of rosewood card tables in the room, probably made by Thomas Seymour of Boston about 1815. Visible through the doorway is a portrait of John F. Kennedy painted by Aaron Shikler in 1970. Under it is a French Empire sofa purchased in 1803 by James Monroe and used by him in the White House. The rug is a wool and cotton reproduction of an early nineteenth-century French Savonnerie carpet.

This oval room on the ground floor, which projects into the bay on the south façade, was the site of President Franklin D. Roosevelt's fireside chats. It serves as an entrance to the White House from the South Grounds for diplomats arriving to present their credentials to the President. Since 1960 the room has been furnished as a drawing room of the Federal period. The wallpaper, entitled "Views of North America," was first printed in 1834 by Jean Zuber et Cie in Rixheim, Alsace, and depicts fanciful American landscapes (the Natural Bridge of Virginia, Niagara Falls, New York Bay,

West Point, and Boston Harbor) based on engravings of the 1820s. The mahogany tall-case clock was made by Effingham Embree of New York in the 1790s; the desk-and-bookcase was made by John Shaw of Annapolis in 1797 and bears his label. The settee is attributed to Abraham Slover and Jacob Taylor, who worked together in New York between 1802 and 1805.

Green Room, The White House. The Green Room has been decorated in shades of green since the Monroe administration. It has had Federal furnishings since the Calvin Coolidge years, but most of the furniture now in place was acquired when the room was extensively refurnished in 1971 as a gift of the Richard King Mellon Foundation. The Carrara mable mantel is one of a pair ordered by President Monroe in 1817 (the other one is now in the Red Room). The gilded New York girandole mirror of about 1820 is decorated with a large American eagle. The mantel is flanked by two mahogany work tables of about 1810 attributed to Duncan Phyfe's shop, as is the mahogany pole screen. An inscription on the frame of the easy chair indicates it was made for Stephen Van Rensselaer of Albany by Phyfe's shop and upholstered in 1811 by Lawrence Ackerman, one of Phyfe's upholsterers. The mahogany-veneer and satinwood desk-and-bookcase of about 1815 is also attributed to Phyfe's shop. Above it hangs *Mosquito Net* by John Singer Sargent, painted about 1908. On the table in the right foreground is a Sheffield-plate coffee urn of about 1785 once owned by John and Abigail Adams. The pair of silver candlesticks, made by a Paris silversmith in 1789, were purchased in 1803 by James Madison, then secretary of state, from James Monroe.

Entrance Hall, The White House, designed by James Hoban, an Irish-born architect living in South Carolina, 1792, Washington, D.C. In the competition held for the design of the President's House, George Washington chose Hoban's design, a simple Palladian building modeled on Leinster House in Dublin, now the Irish National Parliament. Washington supervised the building of the President's House, but he was out of office and had died before it was finished. The gilded beechwood pier table was made in Paris by Pierre Antoine Bellange and is part of a set of furniture ordered by James Monroe from France in 1817. Monroe also ordered the gilt-bronze mantel clock on the table from Paris in the same year. The case, surmounted by a figure of Minerva, was made by Thomire et Cie; the dial is signed by Louis Moinet the elder. The tall gilded English looking glass dates from the late eighteenth century. The bronze light standards were acquired during Theodore Roosevelt's renovation of the White House in 1902.

Opposite

East Room, The White House. This room, designed by Hoban as "the Public Audience" or reception room, has traditionally been used for large gatherings of all sorts. Union troops were quartered in the room during the Civil War, and the bodies of Abraham Lincoln and seven other presidents have lain in state here. The room was not completed until 1829 and was renovated in the present neoclassical style by McKim, Mead and White in 1902. The Steinway piano was presented to Franklin D. Roosevelt in 1938. The portrait of John Quincy Adams in the corner was painted by George P. A. Healy in 1857 and is one of seven portraits of presidents painted by Healy now in the White House.

North Carolina State Capitol, initial design by William
Nichols and his son William Nichols, Jr., in 1833, modified
by Ithiel Town and his partner Alexander Jackson Davis in
1833–34, and executed with further changes by David Paton,
supervising architect, from 1835 to 1840. Except for the
addition of the cast-iron balustrade on the portico in
1859–60, the exterior has remained unchanged since 1840.
Town and Davis added the fully developed porticoes on the
east (shown here) and west fronts and gave the building a
decidedly more Grecian cast. After the capitol had been
under construction for nearly a year and a half, Town
employed the Scottish-born David Paton as the resident
superintendent of construction, and so completely did he
gain the confidence of the building commissioners that early
in 1835 they elected him as the sole architect of the capitol.
The exterior walls are of gneiss, a form of granite, quarried
about a mile from the building site.

Opposite

Senate chamber of the North Carolina State Capitol. The
architects reduced the nearly square interior on the second
and third floors to a stubby Grecian cross by enclosing its
four corners on both floors for offices and anterooms. The
members' seating area is defined by four Ionic columnar
screens and four short, angled walls. These walls support
pendentives which join to form arches and carry a shallow,
coffered dome of lath and plaster. The last architect of the
building, David Paton, who was born in Edinburgh and
trained under Sir John Soane, supervised the building of the
upper portions of the exterior walls, the dome, and all of the
interior of the Capitol. This chamber has obvious precedents
in the Bank of England designed by Soane between 1788
and 1800. The desks and chairs were made by William
Thompson of Raleigh, as were those in the house of
representatives.

Overleaf
Rotunda of the North Carolina State Capitol, Raleigh, built with some modifications from 1833 to 1840. This domed rotunda was constructed at its center to house Antonio Canova's marble statue of George Washington, acquired by the state in 1821. In his neoclassical statehouse, the architect William Nichols combined all the features that thenceforth characterized American state capitols: portico, dome, and rotunda flanked by balanced wings housing the two legislative chambers.

The house of representatives chamber of the North Carolina State Capitol. Modeled after the old House of Representatives chamber (now Statuary Hall) in the United States Capitol, as redesigned and rebuilt by Benjamin Henry Latrobe after the 1814 fire, this room is nearly square. The members sat in an amphitheater defined in the front by a screen of four columns behind the speaker's chair. The coffered, half-domed ceiling springs from a semicircular screen supporting the public gallery. The mahogany desks and chairs were made by William Thompson of Raleigh in 1839 and 1840. The portrait of George Washington is an 1818 copy by Thomas Sully of the Lansdowne portrait by Gilbert Stuart, which was saved from the 1831 fire that destroyed the earlier statehouse.

Stair hall in the east wing of the North Carolina State Capitol. The stair hall extends from the portico to the rotunda on both the first and second floors. The walls of the first- and second-floor passageways throughout the Capitol are faced with smoothly dressed stone.

Opposite
State library on the third floor of the North Carolina State Capitol. The Gothic Revival treatment of the oak-grained tulip woodwork of the state library in this Greek Revival building dates from 1840–41. The shelving, following the marks of the original shelves on the plaster walls, and the arrangements of the books were recreated in the 1970s from surviving documents and invoices to give the conjectured appearance of the room in about 1858. The "Black and Gold Gothic" marble mantel was one of twenty-eight that the firm of J. Struthers and Son of Philadelphia furnished for the Capitol in 1839–40.

The Barker House in Edenton, North Carolina, built in the early 1780s. Edenton is pleasantly situated on a placid bay in Albemarle Sound. In 1722 the "Town on the Fork of Queen Ann's Creek" was incorporated as the capital of the colony and named for Charles Eden, the late governor of the state. The flourishing port of Edenton and its neighboring plantations enjoyed their greatest prosperity in the years preceding the American Revolution. Thomas Barker, the colonial agent for North Carolina in England, returned home to build this commodious house with Federal details and the full-length two-story front porch that was a ubiquitous feature of local domestic architecture.

South façade of Hope Plantation. Stone is believed to have been his own architect when building Hope, a house that is unique in eastern North Carolina architecture in that it can be associated more readily with mansions of eastern seaports than with its own rural environment. Many aspects of its details show a familiarity with Abraham Swan's *British Architect*, published in London in 1745 and reprinted in Philadelphia in 1775. Basically Georgian, the house incorporates a number of neoclassical features so popular in the Federal period. The small building on the left is the original meat house; at the right is a reconstructed dairy.

North façade of Hope Plantation, built by David Stone, about 1800–1803 in Bertie County, in the northeastern part of North Carolina. Known as "the cradle of the colony," the region near the river-port town of Windsor was the first part of North Carolina to be permanently settled. Today it is a land of plantations, farms, pine forests, and small towns. Stone left New England to settle in North Carolina, where he became a leading citizen, a wealthy landowner, merchant, and an ardent patriot. When Elkanah Watson, a noted traveler and diarist, stayed "at Mr. Stone's" in 1786 on a visit to Windsor, he observed that the town had "a genteel society."

Opposite

Central through hall of Hope Plantation. The house was built of pine and cypress, which Stone cut from his own forests and swamplands and hauled to his own sawmill. Above the full, ground-level basement, containing a winter kitchen and storerooms, is the first-floor central hall typical of southern houses. It was used as a living area in the summer, and the family parlor, dining room, and storerooms open off it. The painted canvas floorcloths are adapted from a design in a pattern book on floor decorations published in London in 1739.

240

Family parlor of Hope Plantation. Governor Stone's contemporaries referred to him as a philosopher and toasted him at a celebration in Windsor in 1809 as "a friend of man and a patron of the arts and sciences." During their marriage, the Stones had ten daughters and one son. His estate inventory compiled upon his death in 1818 listed a set of twelve mahogany Federal chairs, as well as a pair of "elegant looking glasses," terrestrial and celestial globes, and a violin. The family parlor would have been used for formal entertaining in the Federal period.

Library of Hope Plantation. Stone graduated from the
College of New Jersey (now Princeton University) in 1788,
during the presidency of the Reverend John Witherspoon,
famous for his emphasis on the "preparation of young men
for dedicated public service." Stone had first shown an
interest in medicine as a profession, but instead read law
and was admitted to the bar in 1790. He held a number of
state political positions, before serving as governor of North
Carolina from 1808 to 1810. Stone is known to have owned
several books on architecture which probably influenced his
designs for the house. The slant-front desk between the
windows was made in Salem, Massachusetts, and was owned
by Stone.

Dining room at Hope Plantation. The walnut corner cupboard of about 1790 is considered one of the finest examples from the shop of the "WH" maker. Above the English silver-plated candlesticks and tea urn hangs an unsigned and undated portrait of Governor Stone. The mid-afternoon dinner was fashionable in the South in the early years of the nineteenth century and the table would have been set without the cloth for the last course of fruit and nuts.

Opposite

Dining room at Hope Plantation. Between the windows is a tall walnut china cupboard of about 1790 attributed to the so-called "WH" maker of the Roanoke River basin, whose work is considered the finest in the area. The rivers and creeks that flow through the northeastern part of North Carolina into Albemarle Sound, provided the earliest form of transportation in the region, supplying the inland port of Edenton, the commercial and social center twenty miles east of Windsor. The mahogany dining table is composed of demilune ends (each with a drop leaf) from a three-piece American dining table of about 1800. Stone had two three-piece dining tables listed in his estate inventory at his death.

Hope Plantation, view from the through hall into Governor and Mrs. Stone's bedroom. Stone's estate inventory lists twelve gray-painted Windsor chairs. The house could have been furnished from a variety of sources: purely utilitarian "plain and neat" furniture made by a local carpenter or cabinetmaker, as well as high-style pieces imported from northern coastal cities.

Edgar Fripp house, known as Tidalholm, Beaufort, South Carolina, built about 1856. A prosperous sea-island cotton planter on Saint Helena Island, Fripp built his large villa in the Italianate style then in vogue. With the wealth that cotton brought, planters built large houses in Beaufort in which to spend summers away from the malarial lowlands. This house, classical in proportion, is oriented to take advantage of prevailing breezes and has large, high-ceilinged rooms. A wide, two-story porch extends along the sides as well as the façade in order to shade windows and doors from the summer sun. Tidalholm was the setting for two movies, *The Great Santini* in 1978 and *The Big Chill* in 1983.

Mulberry Hill, Edenton, North Carolina, built for Clement Blount about 1815. Unquestionably inspired by the prototypes of the Smallwood-Ward and James Washington Bryan houses in New Bern, Blount was evidently determined to reproduce the New Bern architecture on his plantation near Edenton. (His brother, Dr. Frederick Blount was married to Bryan's widow and living in the Bryan house.) In each house, a hall with an arch framing the stair traverses one side, while a pair of large rooms occupies the other. At Mulberry Hill the woodwork in the hall and the mantels and wainscoting are intricately carved with Federal motifs that closely resemble those in the New Bern houses. The effect of verticality and urban sophistication, appropriate for a townhouse, seems incongruous in the rural setting of Mulberry Hill, where the house is surrounded by the meadows and thickets that border the Albemarle Sound.

Marshlands, Beaufort, South Carolina, built about 1814 for Dr. James Robert Verdier. The veranda extends around three sides, and a Palladian window in the rear façade illuminates the stair hall. Elaborate neoclassical mantelpieces made of molded plaster embellish the principal downstairs rooms. The introduction of sea-island cotton from the Bahamas in the 1790s, together with the invention of the cotton gin in 1793, brought unprecedented wealth to Beaufort. This silky, long-staple variety of cotton only grew well in the sandy soil and climate typical of the coastal islands. In the first half of the nineteenth century, one observer found here "a haughty, landed aristocracy, well acquainted with each other, and representing one of the most cultured circles in the South."

Governor's Mansion, atop Arsenal Hill, Columbia, South Carolina, probably designed by George Edward Walker in 1856. The structure destined to become the Governor's Mansion was built as part of the state's Arsenal Military Academy to train officers for the militia. It was built as the officers' quarters in a "good workmanlike manner," according to the building contract, and believed to have been designed by Walker, best known at the time for his design of the library at the College of Charleston. In 1869 the legislature designated "the house on Arsenal Hill" as "a residence for the Governor of the State." The first governor to live there was Robert K. Scott, the first Republican chief executive in the state's history. In 1975 a statewide Fine Arts Commission was established to restore and furnish the Governor's Mansion.

Family dining room of the Governor's Mansion. The Mansion was a "barn of a brick building" by the time that Governor William D. Simpson and his family arrived in 1879. They received a small amount of money from the General Assembly with which to make repairs and furnish the house, and this became the pattern for the next twenty-eight years until 1907, when Governor Martin F. Ansel and his wife began to transform the house into what it is today. Mrs. Ansel began to redecorate the dining room and to acquire appropriate furniture for formal dinners, some of which are still in use to this day.

Large drawing room of the Governor's Mansion. Here visitors are received on official occasions. The table in the foreground is one of a pair attributed to Charles Honoré Lannuier of New York City. The portrait over the late Federal sofa is one of Robert Y. Hayne by Samuel F.B. Morse.

Bedroom at the Governor's Mansion. The mahogany bed
belonged to Arthur Middleton, one of South Carolina's four
signers of the Declaration of Independence, was made in
Charleston and has been attributed to Thomas Elfe, an
eighteenth-century Charleston cabinetmaker. The footposts
are stop-fluted and terminate in plain cabriole legs and
claw-and-ball feet. The Charleston-made mahogany linen
press was made about 1795.

Magnolia Hall, Franklin, Tennessee, built in 1840 by William S. Campbell, a local banker. Franklin is nestled in a slight bend of the picturesque Harpeth River about twenty miles south of Nashville. Throughout the first half of the nineteenth century a prosperous agricultural economy based in large part on cotton guaranteed the success of plantations in the country and prompted the expansion of towns like Franklin. Franklin was established as the seat of the government of Williamson County in 1799. Both the Italianate style of this building and the widow's walk are rarely found in Middle Tennessee.

Opposite

Carriage façade of the Robert Mills Historic House, Columbia, South Carolina, built for Ainsley Hall between 1823 and 1825 and designed by Robert Mills. The elaborate fanlight and side lights around the door are typical of Mills's designs. Ironically, this elegant house was never occupied as a private residence. Ainsley Hall, a leading merchant in Columbia, died before it was finished. His widow was forced to sell it in 1829 to the Presbyterian Theological Seminary; for 101 years the main house served as classrooms, library, and offices. The dependencies have been reconstructed from Mills's plans.

East parlor of the Robert Mills Historic House. The English piano and harp reflect the popularity of these musical instruments of the early nineteenth century. The French Aubusson rug of about 1810 is similar to the one in the west parlor; the English chandelier is the mate to the one there.

Opposite
West parlor of the Robert Mills Historic House. The pair of Grecian sofas is attributed to the workshop of Anthony G. Quervelle of Philadelphia. The mahogany sewing table was probably made in Boston about 1810. The English white marble mantel of about 1790 and the chandelier of about 1810 are not original to the house, but they are similar to those Hall had ordered for the room.

The Plantation Legend

The stereotype of the antebellum South portrays a land of country gentlemen descended from aristocrats who had emigrated from England during the colonial era, living a life of leisure and pleasure regulated by a stern code of conduct and personal honor in a fine two-story Greek Revival mansion. When one thinks of the "typical" Southerner's mansion, it is the Greek Revival image which comes to mind—a symbol of Grecian democracy (which bore some resemblance to democracy in the slave states) adapted from the outward forms of Periclean Athens—a large, two-storied, white temple structure with Doric or Corinthian columns, balustrades on the roofs, and wide piazzas beneath the classical porticoes. The pleasing Greek temple façades contributed to the myth of a "superior culture," that quiet dignity and an atmosphere of harmony and refined taste always existed in the homes of the cotton planters. The popular image of prosperous plantation owners, contented slaves harvesting white cotton fields, and poor rural whites eking out a living on worn-out fields beside a Caldwellian tobacco road—a three-class social structure—is firmly entrenched in the published novels of plantation society by authors such as John Pendleton Kennedy and Beverley Tucker. After the Civil War, impoverished Southerners cherished the romantic legend of a vanished way of life that seems to have been more serene, more unhurried, and closer to nature than the ordeal of Reconstruction. But this image is far from the truth: the letters, diaries, and plantation records that have survived show a great concern for practical affairs, the serenity of the big mansion troubled by the infinite vexations of slavery, and personal worries and sorrows over debt, disease, and death—a region seeking to hold to a way of life that was destined not to endure. The citizens of the beleaguered Cotton Kingdom felt the need to envelop themselves and their region in romantic myths as the sectional controversy came to dominate the American scene; the ultimate results were tragic for both the South and the nation.

In 1860 approximately two-thirds of the agricultural property in Louisiana were farms owned by the "plain folk of the Old South" containing less than one hundred acres which they plowed without the assistance of slave labor. If the romantic ideal of the country gentleman dominated the Old South's image, and even if aristocratic planters possessed an inordinate amount of social prestige and economic power, the largest group of white landowners in the prewar South was, nevertheless, yeoman farmers. The most common agricultural unit was the farm, not the plantation. The legend of the Old South represented a process of simplification and generalization that ignored the infinite variety and fluidity of southern society. Many, but not all, of these middle-class folk owned the less desirable lands, which were less fertile, than those owned by planters—but this mass of southern farmers aspired to be land and slave owners. The history of the Old South is full of success stories of hardworking, horse-trading farmers who became plantation owners. Class consciousness was not great on the part of these people, and they unabashedly moved up the social and economic scale when they were able. Their support of the South's institution of slavery in the wake of abolitionist attacks on it can only be understood in this frame of reference.

The typical small planter lived in an unpretentious, one-story, unpainted clapboard house where his hardworking wife cooked monotonous meals of pork and cornbread, sweetened by sorghum molasses, and boiled the family washing outside in a huge iron pot over an open fire. The southern plantation had a life cycle: in its youth it exhibited many of the characteristics of the frontier, but so rapid was its growth that in the lifetime of the original owner much of the crudeness of the original house either disappeared or was boarded over or replaced by a dignified frame house with white columns supporting a veranda roof. Stumps were removed from fields and rail fences built around the arable fields, and as planters attained wealth they replaced the rough frontier furniture of their houses with polished mahogany. The plantation entered upon old age when its fields became exhausted from ruthless exploitation and then were abandoned as planters moved farther west. The Taits of Georgia, for example, moved in 1819 to the virgin lands of the Alabama River Valley, where with the same labor force they raised twice as much cotton as they had in Georgia. In evaluating antebellum society in the Old South, it should be remembered that much of the hinterland was barely past the frontier stage in the 1840s and 1850s, and the plantations were on land that had been wilderness only a short time before. This was a society of self-made men—businessmen whose business was producing cotton or sugar with slave labor—and the acquisition of increased wealth, that allowed for the possibility of sending a son to college, the leisure for reading Sir Walter Scott's novels, or the means of building an imposing Greek Revival mansion to replace the original practical, indigenous house on the plantation were not realized until the last decade or two before the Civil War.

Mistletoe Plantation, near Natchez, Mississippi, built by John Bisland about 1811, and enlarged by Dr. and Mrs. Matthew Atchison in the late 1840s. The three central bays are part of the original structure, which was composed of four rooms, a central hall, front gallery, and rear loggia. Mistletoe is the earliest of the three plantation houses built by members of the Bisland family; all were within two miles of each other in the area known as Pine Ridge, north of Natchez. John Bisland, a native of Scotland, bought the land in 1803, and according to tradition, built the house as a wedding present for his son, Peter, who married Barbara Foster in 1807. However, during recent repair work a chalk inscription "December 1811" was found on the back of one of the original clapboards at the rear of the house.

Entrance hall of Mistletoe Plantation, built by John Bisland about 1811. Among the unexpected architectural features of this three-bay, four-room cottage are the twelve-foot-six-inch ceilings, the generous windows, comparable to those of the imposing Federal mansions around Natchez, and the substantial side and transom lights. In the rear hall, originally the loggia, is an Empire bookcase made in Natchez, 1830–45, and a slant-top desk of about 1800–1810, also made in Natchez.

Dr. Dubs House in Natchez, Mississippi, built in 1852. This two-story Greek Revival townhouse built by Dr. Charles H. Dubs, a successful dental surgeon from Philadelphia, is one of the finest examples of brickwork in Natchez. Its three bay façade is composed of uniform bricks laid in an all-stretcher pattern with finely cut mortar joints, whereas the remaining walls are laid in a common bond (alternating rows of headers about every eighth row) with common brick. The recessed, grain-painted door with a rectangular transom above is flanked by narrow side lights. The current owners of the house have furnished the house with American decorative arts that range in date from the mid-eighteenth to the mid-nineteenth centuries, with an emphasis on objects made in the lower Mississippi Valley region and particularly furnishings made or owned in Natchez.

Double parlors of the Dr. Dubs House. As is typical of southern Greek Revival townhouses, a long hall extends along one side with double parlors onto it downstairs and bedrooms opening onto it upstairs. Separating the double parlors is a pair of large sliding walnut doors, grain-painted to simulate bird's-eye maple and cypress. In the late eighteenth-century English mahogany corner cupboard are a Liverpool porcelain dessert service and as set of *vieux Paris* porcelain cups, originally used at Homewood Plantation (now demolished) near Natchez. In the center of the front parlor is a mahogany breakfast table with brass inlay and gilded paw feet attributed to Charles Honoré Lanuier of New York City. The early roundabout chair and the later easy chair and sofa all come from New England.

Bedroom in the Dr. Dubs House. The mahogany tall-post bed was made in Massachusetts about 1800 and retains its original grain-painted cornice. Cynthia Atkinson signed the trapunto coverlet and dated it 1816. The looking glass above the marbelized mantel, the andirons, and the fireplace fender are all American from the early nineteenth century. At the right of the fireplace is a New England tiger-maple worktable and to the left, a mahogany dressing table from New York.

Overleaf

Architectural elements from the Shepard-Salisbury Plantation drawing room from a house near Woodville, Mississippi, built by Moses Hook between 1810 and 1818, now in the Anglo-American Art Museum of Louisiana State University in Baton Rouge, Louisiana. The house was named after Salisbury, Massachusetts, Hook's native town, and Charles Moses Shepard, whom Hook's daughter Margaret Ann married in 1829. At the left is a neoclassical desk-and-bookcase of mahogany and inlaid woods made in Baltimore. The fancy Sheraton painted chairs are from New York City, and the green settee with gold painted and stenciled decoration was made in the Boston-Salem region, 1810–20. The mahogany and birch lolling chair is signed by Robert Clark of Newburyport, Massachusetts. Above the settee is a portrait of Captain John Cleves Symmes of New Jersey painted by Thomas Badger about 1820. An army officer stationed in Mississippi and Louisiana, Symmes spent a fortune trying to prove his theory that the earth was made of concentric spheres with people living in each sphere having access to other spheres through apertures at the North and South poles.

Nottoway, near White Castle, Louisiana, on the Mississippi River, designed by Henry Howard for John Hampden Randolph and built between 1857 and 1859. Howard, a native of County Cork, Ireland, was one of the most creative and idiosyncratic of nineteenth-century New Orleans architects. Nottoway is basically in the Italianate style with its conspicuous brackets and square, attenuated columns terminating in jigsaw ornaments and the asymmetrical disposition of the bay, porticos, and wings. Howard extended the twenty-two columns at Nottoway two stories to a height of sixty feet, and in doing so made the house competitive with the great columnar Louisiana plantation houses in the earlier Greek Revival style.

Double parlor or ballroom at Nottoway. With its mixture of Greek Revival and Italianate architectural details, Nottoway is a magnificent hybrid. Nottoway in all its grandeur represents the culmination of the great Louisiana plantation houses built before the Civil War destroyed the prosperity of the region. The floor of the ballroom is maple, while the other floors in the house are cypress. The portrait of Mary Henshaw of Connecticut over the marble mantel is by James Alexander. The pianoforte at the left was made by Thomas Tompkinson in London about 1830.

Opposite
Chrétien Point, near Opelousas, Louisiana, built for Hypolite Chrétien in 1831–32 by Samuel Young and Jonathan Harris. A fine example of the Louisiana neoclassical vernacular style built at the edge of the prairies in the western part of the state. The floor plan of Chrétien Point is still essentially colonial, with contiguous rooms opening directly onto the galleries, but the colossal Tuscan portico pays tribute to the newer Greek Revival style.

Henri Penne House in Iberia Parish, Louisiana, between 1821 and 1830; moved to the Anse La Butte (cove on the hill) district near the town of Breaux Bridge in Saint Martin Parish, Louisiana, in 1974 and there faithfully restored. On the new location, as on the old, the front yard is encircled by live oaks. In addition to the Penne house, the *Petite Maison*, a *pigeonnier*, a storage building, two privies, and a period garden are so arranged to recreate a fairly complete Creole plantation.

Louisiana tall-case clock, made 1830–40, at the Penne House. With a French Morbier movement, the red cypress case was originally grained to resemble mahogany. The clock was first owned by Jacques Dupré, governor of Louisiana in 1830 and 1831.

Opposite

The *salon* of the Penne House. The house was built for Henri Marie Penne, Sr., who was born in Nantes, France, in 1767. One would expect a Louisiana house of this period built for a French-born citizen to reflect many French colonial influences, but there are only two: the principal rooms open directly onto the front gallery, and an exterior staircase leads from the gallery to the half story. The house exhibits more Anglo-American characteristics: the central hall is flanked by two rooms on either side, the double entrance doors have side lights and a glazed transom, and the clapboarded brick-between-posts structure has a gable-end roof and double-hung sash windows. The motif in the center of the *salon* mantel has been furnished in a typically French manner. The furniture in the *salon* is in the Louis Phillippe and French Restauration styles and probably made in New Orleans.

Opposite
Dining room of the Penne House. The mahogany and oak dining table was made in France, about 1830 to 1845, but was found in New Iberia, Louisiana. The fourteen American mahogany fiddle-back chairs of about 1835 are an assembled set of a type that was popular in Louisiana. The table is set with *vieux Paris* porcelain collected locally. The pelmets over the windows are made of an antique French silk and cotton fabric.

View from the gallery of the *Petite Maison* into the *salon* of the Penne House. The complex of detached and semi-detached buildings here affords a rare glimpse into the setting that might commonly have been lived in by southwestern Louisiana Creole planters in the 1820s and 1830s.

Arcadian bedroom of the Penne house. The low-post bed of 1830–40 is from Saint Landry Parish, Louisiana, and reflects the blending of Anglo-American and French Louisiana characteristics. The basic style is Anglo-American, but the poles supporting mosquito nets and the use of swamp maple, ash, and cypress for the woods are Arcadian. The Arcadian quilt on the bed was woven from white, indigo-dyed, and natural yellow cotton threads in different and fairly complex patterns. The pine and birch cradle at the foot of the bed is French Canadian but was found in Baton Rouge. In the foreground is a copy of volume 11 of Denis Diderot's *Encyclopédie* (1772), with illustrations of looms and the tools needed for weaving.

Bedroom of the *Petite Maison,* on the property of the Penne House. The portrait of Alexandre De Vins Bienvenu II, painted in New Orleans by an unidentified artist, is accompanied by a Louisiana cherry armoire of about 1810 inlaid with Bienvenu's monogram. The high-post mahogany bed of about 1820 was found in Saint Landry Parish.

Poydras-Holden House on Bayou Chenal near Baton Rouge, Louisiana, the earliest section built before 1790, the house raised on brick piers before the mid-1820s. The house is evocative of Creole Louisiana—the French and Spanish colonial milieu of the late and early nineteenth centuries, when such raised cottages were to be seen on plantations along the Mississippi and the adjacent streams and bayous. This late eighteenth-century house, originally owned by Julien de Lallande Poydras, who was born in France and became a distinguished planter, was moved eleven miles in 1975 from New Roads, Louisiana, to the site of a former sugar plantation by Dr. and Mrs. Jack Holden. As is characteristic of French venacular building practices, neither the façade nor the placement of the colonettes of the porch is symmetrical. The walls are framed with cypress and then filled with *bousillage*, a mixture of mud and moss or other binding material. As was typical, the house is surrounded by a fence of split planks (*pieux*) and set in a pasture.

Main room of the Poydras-Holden House. The room has a ten-and-one-half foot ceiling and double doors opening both onto both the front and back galleries. The prominent chimney piece and mantel are part of the mid-1820s alterations. John Pintard, a New York City merchant who visited New Orleans and its surroundings in 1801, noted: "Pictures either portrait paintings or engravings are very rare excepting over the chimney piece, which is always finished with a mirror and a painting above, inserted in the panel work." In this case, the subject is a member of the Fabacher family of New Orleans, painted in the early 1850s by an unknown artist. The armoire was probably made in the late 1790s for Suzanne Bosseron Fortin, who owned it, or for her father, François Bosseron, a merchant in Indiana in the late eighteenth century. The family moved to Louisiana from Vincennes, Indiana, where the armoire was made in 1802 or 1803. The walnut tables and the armchair at the right are of Louisiana origin.

Garden in the front of the Poydras-Holden House. John Pintard of New York, visiting New Orleans and environs in 1801, wrote that gardens were "disposed in the old still formal style—the border and circles kept up with strips of board" as is the case at Poydras. The dovecote, or *pigeonnier*, of about 1829, a typical Louisiana plantation outbuilding, was moved from Natchitoches, Louisiana, and has *bousillage* walls. The culture of the Louisiana Creoles paralleled to some extent and was intertwined with that of the Acadians in southwestern Louisiana. Of French descent, the Acadians first settled in Canada in the eighteenth century and came to French settlements in Louisiana during and after the Seven Years War (1756–63). Living in rural areas and in relative isolation, the descendants of the Acadians tenaciously retained their language and many of their traditions, including growing, spinning, and weaving cotton in textiles for home consumption. Examples of Acadian fabrics are found throughout this house.

286

Mount Hope, a cottage built in Baton Rouge, Louisiana, by Joseph Sharp between 1795 and 1817. The deep veranda on the front and both sides is raised a few feet from the ground on brick piers. The front door with a transom and side lights is spacious and simple, as are the architectural details throughout the house. Mount Hope is typical of the early cottage-style plantation houses in the region.

Parlor at Mount Hope, Baton Rouge. The name of
Louisiana's capital city, Baton Rouge, originated at the
beginning of the eighteenth century from a place on a bluff
where "there is a post painted red that the savages have
sunk there to mark the land line between the two nations."
The large Philadelphia settee in the parlor at Mount Hope
was made about 1825. The small desk of about 1830 is
thought to be a Southern piece. The portrait of a boy above
the desk is by the English history painter John Opie, and the
nineteenth-century English clock in the corner is inscribed
in the face, *R.H. Sutcliffe, Horseforth*.

Clinton Courthouse, East Feliciana Parish, Louisiana, built
in 1839–40 in the Greek Revival style with striking
affinities to several neighboring plantation houses.
Surrounded by twenty-eight Doric columns which support an
exceptionally wide entablature, the courthouse is a square
building with stuccoed brick walls and a hipped roof
crowned with an overscaled cupola. Like so many of the
neoclassical houses of Louisiana, the Clinton Courthouse is
not, strictly speaking, in the Greek Revival style. It has no
pediment and the attenuated columns are more Roman than
Greek. While working on his *Birds of America*, John James
Audubon composed a lyrical tribute to the Feliciana country
of Louisiana: "It is where the Great Magnolia shoots up its
majestic trunk, crowned with evergreen leaves, and
decorated with a thousand beautiful flowers, that perfume
the air around; where forest and fields are adorned with
blossoms of every hue; where the golden orange ornaments
the gardens and groves . . . where berries and fruits of all
descriptions are met with at every step."

Greek Revival: A National Style

The Greek Revival shared with the earlier Federal or neoclassical movement its basic intentions, aesthetic attitudes, and in some cases even a continuity of architects and craftsmen. It became the dominant national style between 1820 and 1860, and flourished especially in the Deep South of the slaveowners. The enthusiasm for Greek independence early in this period; the emphasis on the classics in a gentleman's education; and the fact that the Greek temple form was a symbol of Grecian democracy, which could be interpreted to rationalize slavery, all combined to make the style popular in the southern states. However, the overtones became more complex, reflecting the diverging sectional attitudes emerging in American society. New Englanders might translate Homer, Sophocles, and Aristotle to show what heights humanitarianism had reached in the past and might, with proper application, be reached again. Southerners would scan Plato's *Republic* for proof that slavery, and slavery alone, was the system which could make such a culture possible. "The pronounced drift of Southern thought, in the years immediately preceding the Civil War, toward the ideal of a Greek democracy," Vernon Parrington has said, "was no vagrant eddy but a broadening current of tendency."

The Greek Revival was also an architecture of brilliant response to the environmental demands of a warm semi-tropic climate: the stilted pavilion form; the huge, light parasol roof and perimetric galleries; the large door and window openings, tall ceilings, and through ventilation; the jalousie to solve the paradox of privacy and ventilation; and in the city, the patio, loggia, and courtyard garden. Since the planters entertained often, some of the estates had *garçonniers,* small classical outbuildings separate from the mansion house which provided quarters for the children and guests. These upper-class Southerners adapted the outward forms of the plantation Greek Revival style to the practical needs of an indigenous idiom to form the richest and most viable of all our regional architectures, so that, as Oliver Larkin has phrased it, "under their colonnades and pediments they had created something which the Greeks never knew."

The geometric simplicity and revealed structure of the Greek Revival seemed to lend itself to translation in wood, and even the provincial carpenter using the ancient vocabulary in building a traditional country house was capable of achieving a naïve but forthright statement of true dignity. There had always been a wide and eager audience for the standard handbooks, carpenters' guides, and architectural plates of British publishers, and it was not long before similar works began to appear on this side of the Atlantic. Especially successful were the books of plates by the architects Asher Benjamin, *The Practice of Architecture* (1833), and Minard Lafever, *The Beauties of Modern Architecture* (1835), both treatises of which extolled the Greek style. In New England, Benjamin reigned, but the rest of the country down through the Gulf States was all Lafever country. By the time of the Civil War, the Greek Revival had permeated from the high style through the low style to the folk level of American architecture and had extended to every corner of the land. Adopted by the common man as well as the professional architect, the bookish Greek idiom became the first building style in American history to be consciously understood and embraced as a truly national mode of building, giving the architecture of Jacksonian American a remarkable homogeneity and a high degree of competence. The excellence of vernacular craftsmanship during this period was due to the skill of its artisans, but the sophistication of design often found in remote regions is traceable to the pattern books.

An astonishing number of new American towns that lay west of the Appalachian mountains were given Greek placenames during this period—towns that had Greek architecture as well as Greek names. Even though Talbot Hamlin has documented ten architects by name in the frontier town of St. Louis with a population of less than 6,000 in 1821 when Missouri was admitted to the Union, many buildings in the Mississippi Valley remain anonymous, the work of carpenters depending on handbooks and local building traditions. What distinguishes provincial Greek Revival architecture in America from the rational neoclassical movement is a persistent bookishness, a much stricter adherence to the proportions and character of the Greek orders and the Greek ornamental system. Yet inventiveness and freedom are to be seen on the frontier vernacular level, where the anonymous builder was so utterly committed to wood, all the while aspiring to change the familiar material into forms which he admired but never really quite understood. In spite of its appealing simplicity and strength, the pure temple form was not the most common in American house design. Far more prevalent was the pedimented temple block with side wings in which the mass remains axis of the building, which offered greater variety in appearance and internal arrangements—severely classical in its symmetry, yet varied in the unwavering clarity of its profile. Much of Greek Revival architecture—from the plantation to the folk level—produced buildings of a high order: functional, inventive, refined, and skillful in execution. These architects and builders were progressive in their use of new materials and techniques—the development of the wooden truss which made possible the erection of railroad and covered bridges, and "balloon frame" construction devised in the 1830s as a result of mass-produced and standardized lumber and cheap nails which revolutionized wooden-house construction. Yet, with all its functional innovations, Greek Revival architecture in America still remained revivalist and romantic.

The Greek Revival was not only a chaste and simple style, which suited well the prevailing mood of a "common man" culture. Having originated in the democracies of ancient Greece, it was regarded by most Americans as an appropriate symbol of the political ideals and cultural aspirations upon which their nation was based. With Jackson's inauguration, the first commoner to hold the office of President of the United States (whose own house, The Hermitage, was built near Nashville in the Greek style), the middle class frontier of western agrarianism emerged and triumphed as a driving force of American democracy. The way was now open for the building of the West, with the identification of the past with the present, of the noble simplicity, calm grandeur, and ethical harmony of a Grecian utopia with Jacksonian America. The heartland of the New World was no part of the old Roman empire. Americans did not, like Europeans, travel over highways originally laid down for the legions of Caesar, nor in the midst of towns or on some nearby hill see ruined temples from the time when Zeus was the father of gods and men. But by 1832 when Samuel F. Smith wrote "My Country, 'Tis of Thee," he referred to the "templed hills" that were by then already so characteristic of the American landscape. Buildings were painted "the whitest of white," wrote Charles Dickens, recalling the gleaming marble of ancient temples. Tocqueville was delighted by the sight of such "little palaces of white marble" until he learned they were whitewashed brick and painted wood.

Americans gave their new villages and towns classical names such as Rome, Troy, Athens, Syracuse, Ithaca, Utica, Alexandria, and Demopolis, and lived on streets sometimes known as Euclid Avenue, Appian Way, Arcadia Drive, or Phaeton Road. Constitutionally we are not a democracy but a republic; that is, a *res publica*,

294

a phrase referring to the commonwealth of a government by elected representatives. The head of the government is a president, from *praesidens;* the national legislature is a congress, from *congressus,* a coming together; and the upper house is a senate, from *senatus,* a gathering of older and presumably wiser men. The congress meets in a capitol, a word originally designating a citadel or temple on a hilltop, like the temple of Jupiter Optimus Maximus which stood on the Capitoline Hill in Rome. Our first two political parties were Federalists and Republicans, terms originating in the Latin language; our present ones are Republicans and Democrats, the second term coming from the Greek. Even today, when Greek and Latin have disappeared from most public education, many of our liveliest political words are from the Latin, as in the cases of quota, moratorium, referendum, and propaganda. Our decimal coinage, largely the creation of Jefferson, used classical iconography that has long persisted of the eagle on one side and on the other the female figure of the goddess of Liberty, Justice, Columbia, or Prosperity (her costume classical) surrounded by symbols of agriculture or manufacture.

The birth of this new independent republic in the New World rejuvenated classical symbolism—the feeling and belief that a great romantic revival of the best ages of Greece and Rome was possible—and created a new mythology, part of it local to the United States, part of it appealing generally to the Old World. As these romantic dreamers idealized the past, they conceived an Athens and Rome that never existed and in their own version of the ancient world created a vocabulary and iconography that served as a new language for the republican hope of man. They commonly shared in the spirit of the age a sentimental preference for nostalgia and escapism over contact with the coarse fact of reality. This sense of striving, this surge after something just out of reach, this romantic yearning to pass beyond experience is what separates the nineteenth century from the eighteenth. These tendencies, susceptible to emotional as well as intellectual judgments, developed in literature into what Howard Mumford Jones has labeled "romantic Hellenism," and in Greek Revival architecture what William H. Pierson, Jr. has termed "Romantic Classicism."

Classicism and the Decorative Arts

The Greek Revival became a ubiquitous and decidedly Americanized style that complemented the furniture and furnishings made in what is commonly called the Empire style. The "Grecian" or "modern" style, as it was known to its contemporaries, introduced the actual use of ancient furniture forms as they were represented in the pattern books of Napoleon Bonaparte's French Empire and the roughly parallel versions of the English Regency. By the third and fourth decades of the nineteenth century, the delicate grace and slender proportions of the Federal style became progressively heavier and coarser in character, giving way to a massive solidity that was a symptom of decline. Charles Percier and Pierre Fontaine, in their *Recueil des décorations intérieures,* published in 1801, were the first to illustrate examples in the new archaeological style. Three years later Napoleon made the pair his official court architects and decorators, and from this eminent post they influenced the direction of furniture design through French classicism throughout the western world. Thomas Hope, in his *Household Furniture and Interior Decoration* (1807), one of the first English equivalents of these archaic designs, expressly acknowledged his debt to the earlier work of Percier and Fontaine. This pair of Frenchmen by no means restricted themselves to reproductions of Greek forms depicted on pottery, gravestones, and wall paintings but used whatever ancient sources—Roman, Etruscan, Egyptian, as well as Greek—they could adapt to satisfy the needs and vanities of Napoleon and his imperial court. The Greek klismos-form chair, distinguished by the graceful sweep of the back and a broad curvilinear crest rail, was and still is a perfectly comfortable and handsome seating form. Another variety of chair with the "Grecian cross" or curule legs, based on a Roman magistrate's folding chair. Greco-Roman tripods suggested new shapes for tables and candlestands. Other supports took the form of the monopode (creatures having only one foot) and winged female caryatid figures. Chair, sofa, and table legs in the nature of a winged lion's paws, hock-footed animal supports terminating in paw feet, swans and dolphins, and stylized curves of anthemia and scrolls, and all manner of inlaid, applied, painted, and stenciled gilt ornament traced their designs to classical sources.

French influence, however direct or indirect, was clear in much of the furniture made in America in this period. And as French fashions evolved, they were widely publicized through the designs published by Pierre de la Mésangère in *Collection des Meubles et Objets de Goût,* which appeared serially in Paris between 1796 and 1830. Relying heavily on large expanses of richly figured "matchbook" mahogany veneers for ornamentation on large case pieces such as the *secrétaire à abattant* and the *bonheur du jour* (small secretary bookcase designed for ladies' use), these pieces reflect the heavier, more architectonic style of the French Restoration. The bulkiness of form and heaviness of detail that became so prevalent and, ultimately, exaggerated in the late Empire period as the style reached its climax in the 1830s. The rich medley of carving and gilded decoration of the late Empire style was ultimately to be replaced by the extensive "pillar and scroll" production, with broad surfaces often veneered with mahogany and rosewood. The ubiquitous symbol of this new fashion was the bold scroll support made in square section and used in various combinations on sofas, tables, and case pieces. The geometric simplicity of the pillar and scroll style was first illustrated in America in a widely circulated advertisement of 1833 by Joseph Meeks and Sons, cabinetmakers of New York. Finally published for furniture manufacturers everywhere by John Hall, the architect-designer of Baltimore in *The Cabinet Makers Assistant* (1840) the pillar and scroll form remained in vogue for decades from Boston to New Orleans. Hall asserted that "novelty, simplicity and practicability, are blended with the present designs, in which originality mostly prevails. . . . As far as possible, the style of the United States is blended with European taste, and a graceful outline and simplicity of parts are depicted in all the objects."

By this time the classical ancestry of these forms was almost completely lost in the "blend" of influences and the "simplicity of parts," yet in scale and design such pieces admirably complemented the fashionable Greek Revival interiors. In reviewing the history of furniture in connection with the New York Crystal Palace exhibition of 1853, Benjamin Silliman, Jr., the eminent Yale professor, would look back on what he considered the "ponderous and frigid monstrosities" of the Federal and Empire styles. "The solemn affectation of Greek and Roman forms was so ridiculous," he observed, "that only the inherent vitality and grand simplicity of the classic motives [motifs] enabled them to survive 'the deep damnation of this *taking off.*'" Taste was changing, as it constantly does, but the classical style had endured longer than any other style that was to follow in America.

Acknowledgments

The author's indebtedness is large. I owe a particular debt of gratitude to my colleagues at Sotheby's and *The Magazine ANTIQUES*, an extraordinarily stimulating assembly of friends and professionals for their camaraderie and counsel. Their imaginative encouragement and endless forbearance, in ways and means they can hardly realize, have been of indispensable help. They are at Sotheby's: Betty Byrns, Nancy Druckman, Laura Evans, Leslie Keno, Peter Lang, Letitia Roberts, Katherine Ross, Larry Sirolli, Nancy Smith, William Stahl, and Alexandra Watkins; and at *ANTIQUES*: Elizabeth Cafferty, Eleanor Gustafson, Allison Ledes, and Alfred Mayor. The preparation of this volume would have been impossible without the friendly collaboration of Paul Rocheleau, a consummate master of photography, and the splendid images of two other longtime friends, George Fistrovich and Arthur Vitols—their eye for detail and passion for precision have added immensely to the style of the book. Thanks are due to David Larkin for his invaluable work in the selection and layout of the photographs; his inspired contribution is far greater than the single line on the verso of the title page would indicate. I should also like to thank with deep appreciation Lois Brown and Elizabeth White at Rizzoli for preparing the manuscript for the press with unflagging optimism, enthusiastic support, and the highest of editorial standards.

Finally, I owe to the late Howard Mumford Jones of Harvard University a passage from a book by Charles Leslie, published in London in 1700, *A Defence of a book intituled: The snake in the grass*, which I quote here because it is too delightful not to be rescued from oblivion: "I must trouble the reader to correct the errata of the press, as he finds them. For I am quite tyr'd."

Select Bibliography

Adams, William Howard, ed. *The Eye of Thomas Jefferson*. 1976.

Albion, Robert G. *The Rise of New York Port, 1815–1860*. 1939.

Browne, Gary L. *Baltimore in the Nation, 1789–1861*. 1980.

Cochran, Thomas C. *Frontiers of Change: Early Industrialism in America*. 1981.

Cooper, Wendy A. *In Praise of America: American Decorative Arts, 1650–1830/Fifty Years of Discovery Since the 1929 Girl Scouts Loan Exhibition*. 1980.

Cornelius, Charles Over. *Furniture Masterpieces of Duncan Phyfe*. 1922; reprint, 1970.

Craig, Lois, ed. *The Federal Presence: Architecture, Politics, and Symbols in United States Government Buildings*. 1978.

Dangerfield, George. *The Awakening of American Nationalism, 1815–1828*. 1965.

Davidson, Marshall B., ed. *The American Heritage History of American Antiques: From the Revolution to the Civil War*. 1968.

Fales, Dean A., Jr. *American Painted Furniture 1660–1880*. 1972.

Fitch, James Marston. *American Building: The Historical Forces That Shaped It*. 1973.

Garvan, Beatrice B. *Federal Philadelphia, 1785–1825: The Athens of the Western World*. 1987.

Gilchrist, David T., ed. *The Growth of the Seaport Cities, 1790–1825*. 1967.

Gowans, Alan. *Images of American Living: Four Centuries of Architecture and Furniture as Cultural Expression*. 1964; new edition, 1976.

Hamlin, Talbot. *Greek Revival Architecture in America*. 1944.

Hammond, Bray. *Banks and Politics in America: From the Revolution to the Civil War*. 1957.

Hewitt, Benjamin A., Patricia E. Kane, and Gerald W. R. Ward. *The Works of Many Hands: Card Tables in Federal America, 1790–1820*. 1982.

Honour, Hugh. *Neo-Classicism*. Middlesex, England, 1968.

Kirk, John T. *American Furniture and the British Tradition to 1830*. 1982.

Laurie, Bruce. *Artisans into Workers: Labor in Nineteenth-Century America*. 1989.

Lindstrom, Diane. *Economic Development in the Philadelphia Region, 1810–1850*. 1978.

Mahoney, Timothy R. *River Towns in the Great West: The Structure of Provincial Urbanization in the American Midwest, 1820–1870*. 1989.

Matthews, Jean V. *Toward a New Society: American Thought and Culture, 1800–1830*. 1991.

McClelland, Nancy. *Duncan Phyfe and the English Regency, 1795–1830*. 1939; reprint, 1980.

McWhiney, Grady. *Cracker Culture: Celtic Ways in the Old South*. 1988.

Montgomery, Charles F. *American Furniture: The Federal Period in the Henry Francis du Pont Winterthur Museum*. 1966.

O'Brien, Michael. *Rethinking the South: Essays in Intellectual History*. 1988.

Owsley, Frank L. *Plain Folk of the Old South*. 1949.

Pierson, William H., Jr. *American Buildings and Their Architects: The Colonial and Neoclassical Styles*. 1970.

Pred, Allan R. *Urban Growth and the Circulation of Information: The United States System of Cities, 1790–1840*. 1973.

Quimby, Ian M. G., and Polly Anne Earl, eds. *Technological Innovation and the Decorative Arts*. 1974.

Rock, Howard B. *Artisans of the Young Republic: The Tradesmen of New York City in the Age of Jefferson*. 1979.

Scherer, John L. *New York Furniture at the New York State Museum*. 1984.

Sellers, Charles. *The Market Revolution: Jacksonian America, 1815–1846*. 1991.

Shaw, Ronald E. *Erie Water West: A History of the Erie Canal, 1792–1854*. 1966.

Smelser, Marshall. *The Democratic Republic, 1801–1815*. 1968.

Stoneman, Vernon C. *John and Thomas Seymour: Cabinetmakers in Boston, 1794–1816*. 1959.

Summerson, John. *The Classical Language of Architecture*. 1967.

Swan, Mabel M. *Samuel McIntire, Carver, and the Sandersons, Early Salem Cabinet Makers*. 1934.

Tracy, Berry B., and William H. Gerdts. *Classical America, 1815–1845*. 1963.

Ward, Gerald W. R., ed. *Perspectives on American Furniture*. 1988.

Warner, Sam Bass, Jr. *The Private City: Philadelphia in Three Periods of Its Growth*. 1968.

Watts, Steven. *The Republic Reborn: War and the Making of Liberal America, 1790–1820*. 1987.

Weidman, Gregory R. *Furniture in Maryland, 1740–1940: The Collection of the Maryland Historical Society*. 1984.

Weigley, Russell F., ed. *Philadelphia: A 300-Year History*. 1982.

Wilentz, Sean. *Chants Democratic: New York City and the Rise of the American Working Class, 1788–1850*. 1984.

Wyatt-Brown, Bertram. *Southern Honor: Ethics and Behavior in the Old South*. 1982.

Zenvin, Robert Brooke. *The Growth of Manufacturing in Early Nineteenth Century New England*. 1975.

Places of Interest

Many of the houses illustrated in this book welcome visitors. They either have official hours when they are open, or they can be seen by appointment.

Photo Credits

The photographs are by Paul Rocheleau except for the following: